GUITAR TAB 2012 2013

AUTHENTIC TRANSCRIPTIONS WITH NOTES AND TABLATURE

Music transcriptions by Pete Billmann, Addi Booth, and David Stocker

ISBN 978-1-4803-4070-1

HAL•LEONARD®
CORPORATION

7777 W. BLUEMOUND RD. P.O. BOX 13819 MILWAUKEE, WI 53213

Visit Hal Leonard Online at
www.halleonard.com

The A Team

Words and Music by Ed Sheeran

*Symbols in parentheses represent chord names respective to capoed guitar.
Symbols above reflect actual sounding chords. Capoed fret is "0" in tab. Chord symbols reflect overall harmony.

**5th & 6th strings only.

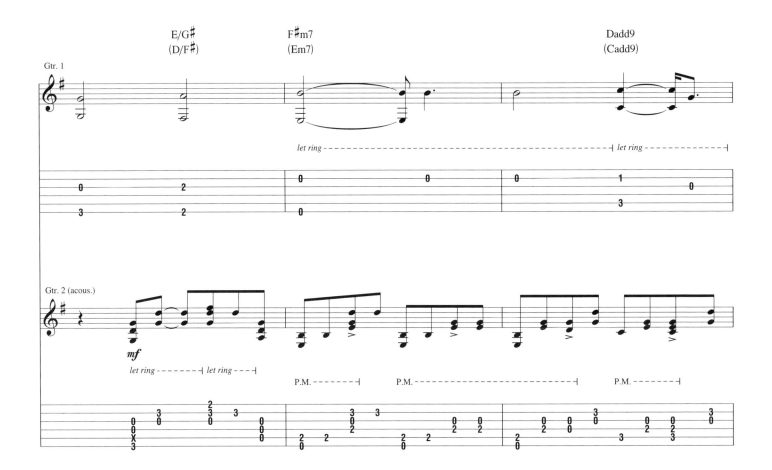

Verse

1. White lips, ___

pale face ___ breath-ing in ___ snow - flakes. ___

3

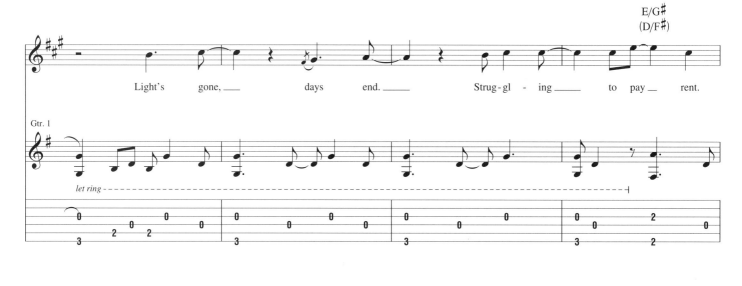

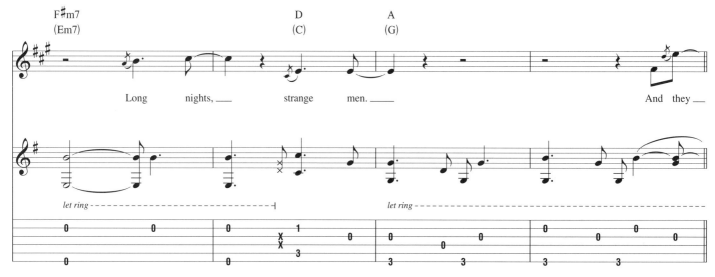

4

Pre-Chorus

say __ she's in the Class __ A __ Team, stuck in her __ day-

-dream. Been this way __ since eight - een. __ But late - ly __ her

Interlude

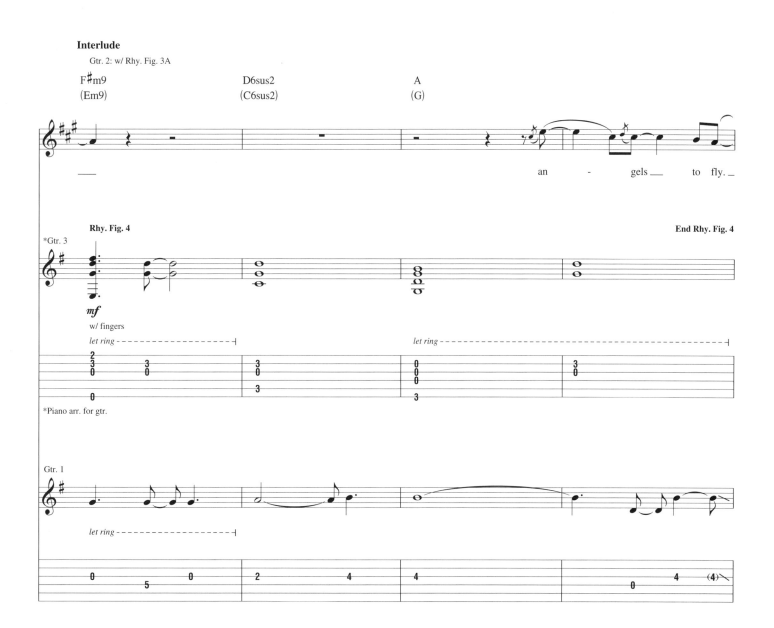

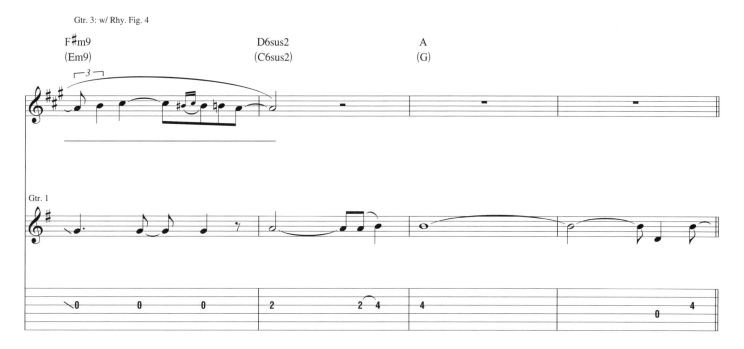

Verse

Gtr. 2: w/ Rhy. Fig. 1 (2 times)

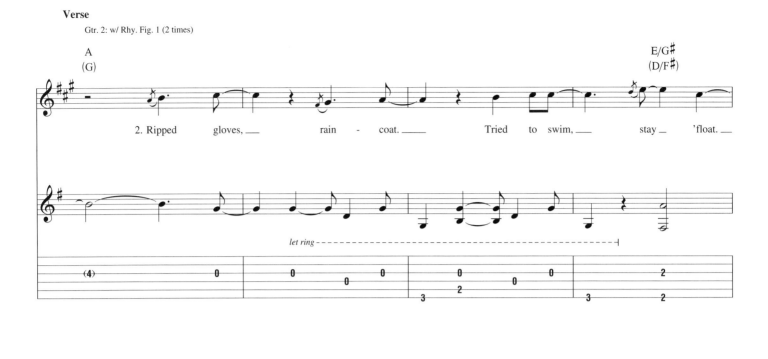

2. Ripped gloves, __ rain - coat. __ Tried to swim, __ stay __ 'float. __

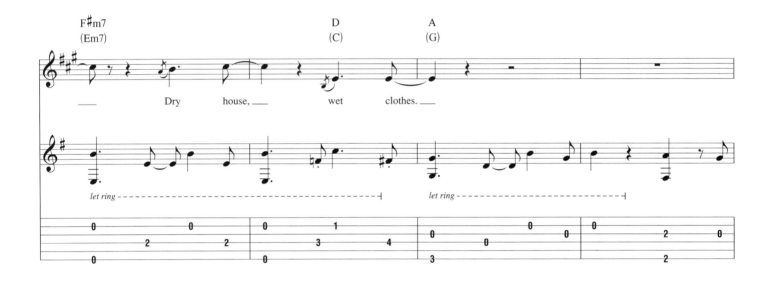

__ Dry house, __ wet clothes. __

Loose change, __ bank notes. __ Wea - ry - eyed, __ dry __ throat.

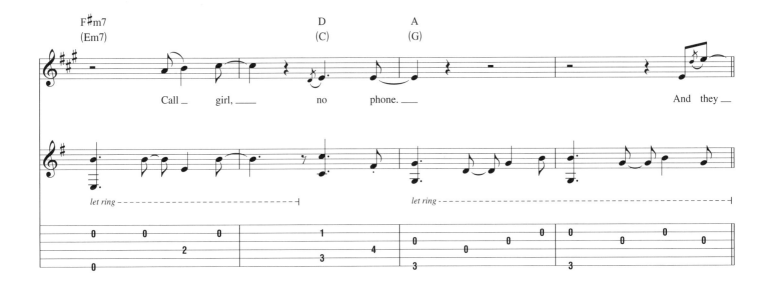

Call __ girl, __ no phone. __ And they __

Pre-Chorus

Gtr. 2: w/ Rhy. Fig. 2 (2 times)

__ say __ she's in the Class __ A __ Team, stuck in her __ day-

-dream. Been this way __ since eight - een. __ But late - ly __ her face __

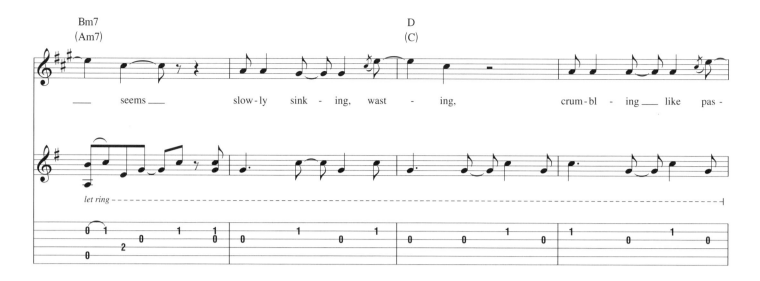

D.S. al Coda

Coda

Bridge

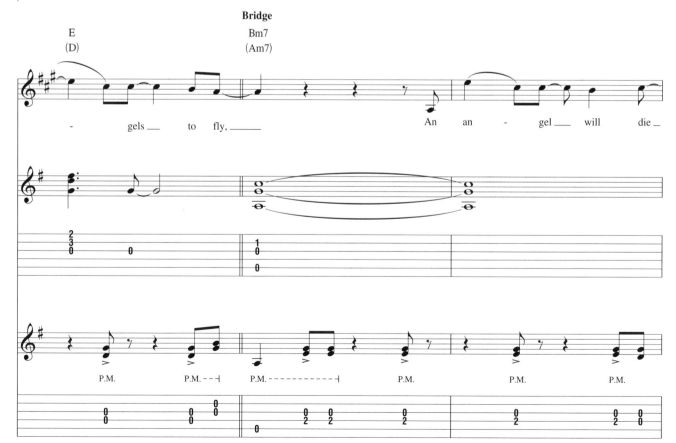

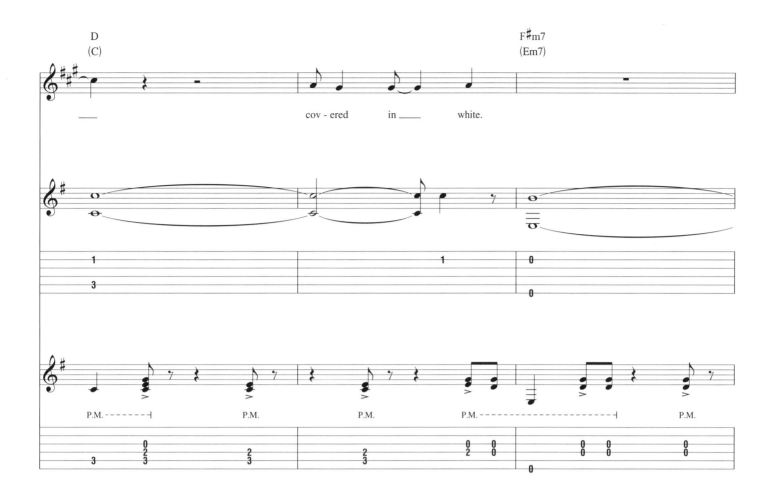

Guitar Solo

Bkgd. Voc.: w/ Voc. Fig. 1
Gtr. 1: w/ Rhy. Fig. 3
Gtr. 2: w/ Rhy. Fig. 3A (1st 4 meas.)

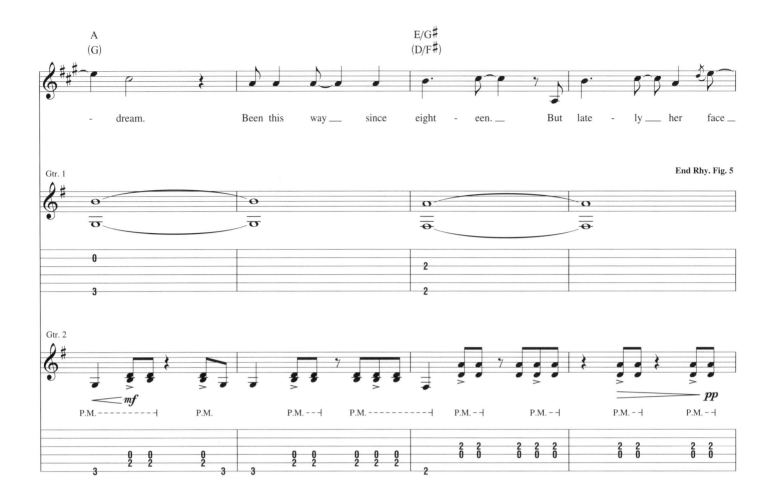

-dream. Been this way since eight - een. But late - ly her face

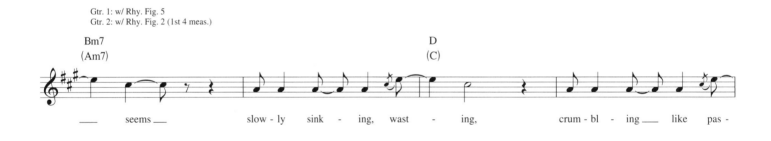

_ seems _ slow - ly sink - ing, wast - ing, crum - bl - ing _ like pas -

-tries. _ They _ scream, _ the worst _ things in _ life come free to us. And we're

Chorus

Bkgd. Voc.: w/ Voc. Fig. 1 (3 times)
Gtr. 2 tacet

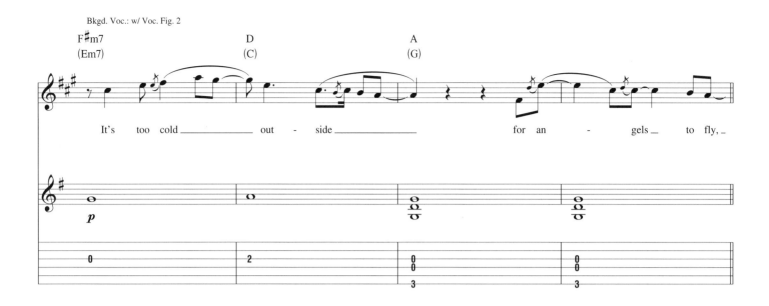

It's too cold _____ out - side _____ for an - gels _ to fly, _

Outro

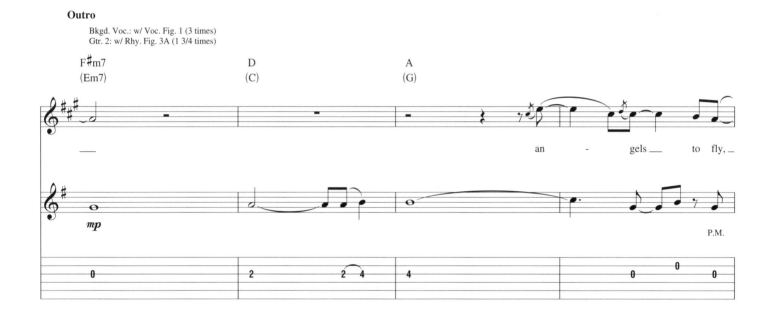

an - gels _ to fly, _

P.M.

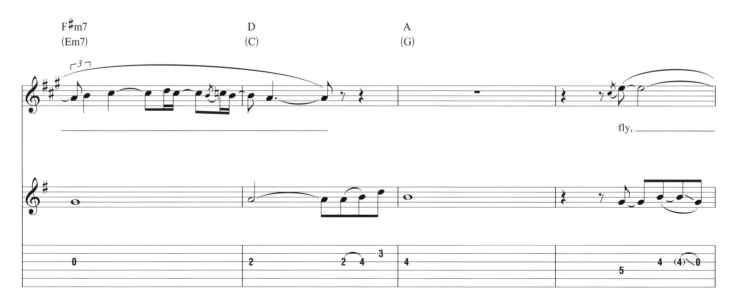

fly, _____

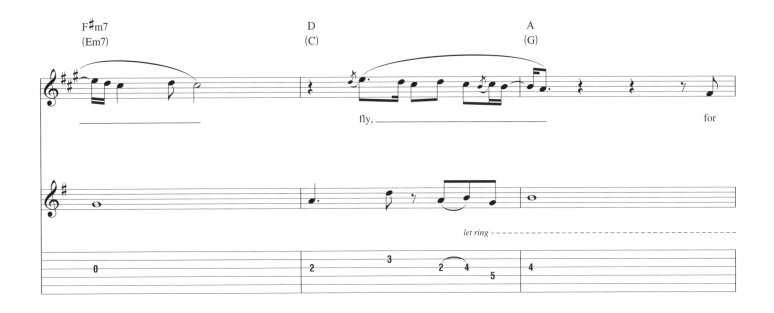

Bkgd. Voc.: w/ Voc. Fig. 2

Bully

Words and Music by Three Days Grace and Barry Stock

Drop D tuning, down 1 step:
(low to high) C-G-C-F-A-D

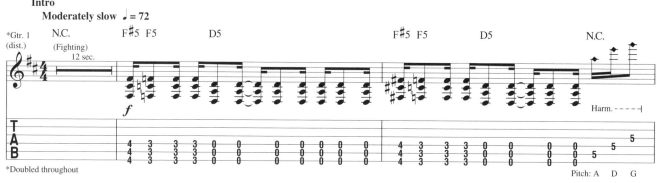

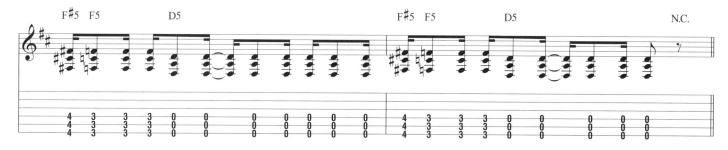

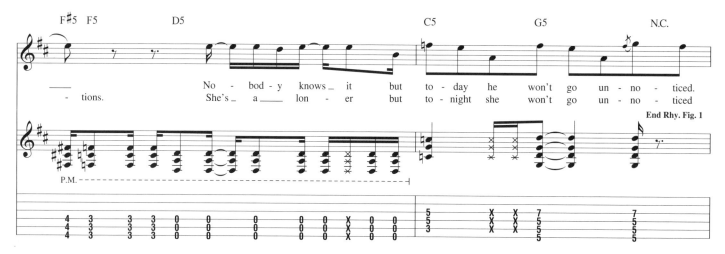

Gtr. 1: w/ Rhy. Fig. 1

He ___ can't for - get, can't for - give ___ for what they said. ___
if she ___ can't re - mem - ber when she los - es her tem - per. ___

___ He's nev - er been so ___ hurt, but to - day the scream - ing is o - ver.
___ No - bod - y knows ___ her, but to - night the si - lence is o - ver.

%% Chorus

Blame the fam - i - ly. ___   Blame the bul - ly. ___   Blame it on ___ me. ___

Gtr. 2 (dist.)

mf

Gtr. 3 (dist.)

mf

Gtr. 1

f

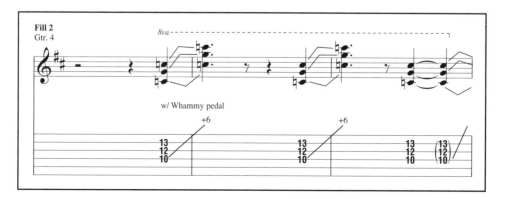

3rd time, Gtr. 4: w/ Fill 2

C5   G5   F5 G5   A5 G5 F5 E♭5 F♯5 E♭5 D5   F5 G5   A5 G5 F5 E♭5 F♯5 E♭5 D5

May-be {1. he / 2. she / 3. they} need - ed   to be want-ed. Blame the fam - i - ly. _____   Blame the bul - ly. _____

Fill 2
Gtr. 4

w/ Whammy pedal

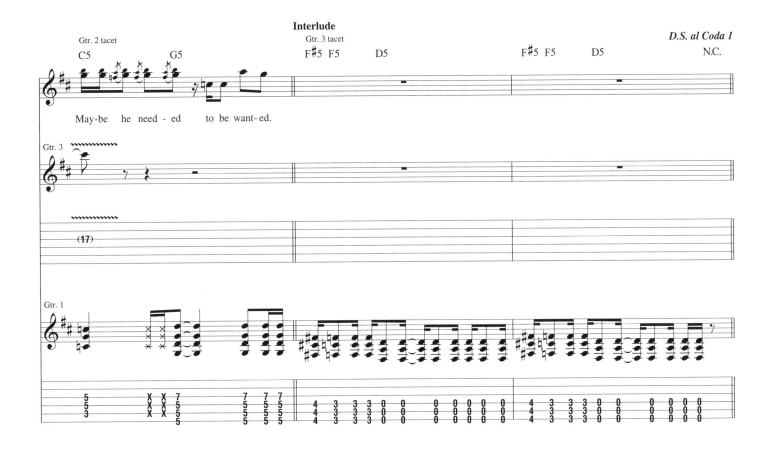

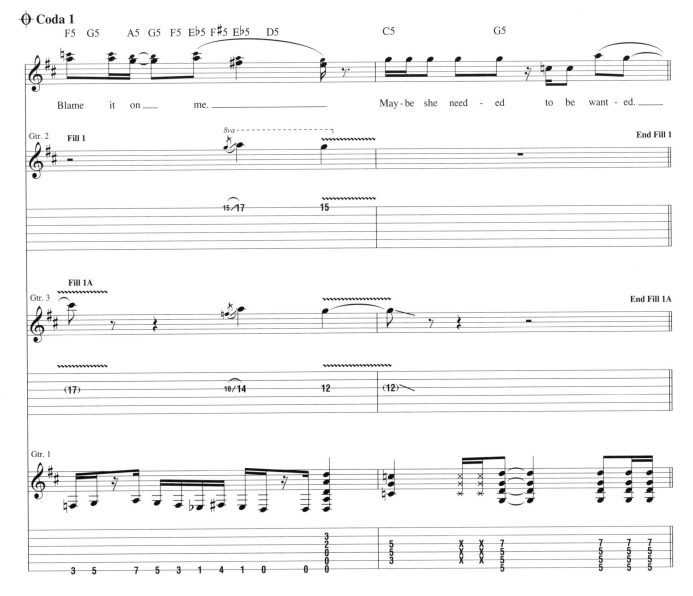

Interlude

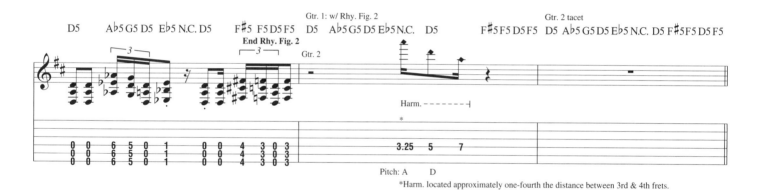

*Harm. located approximately one-fourth the distance between 3rd & 4th frets.

Bridge

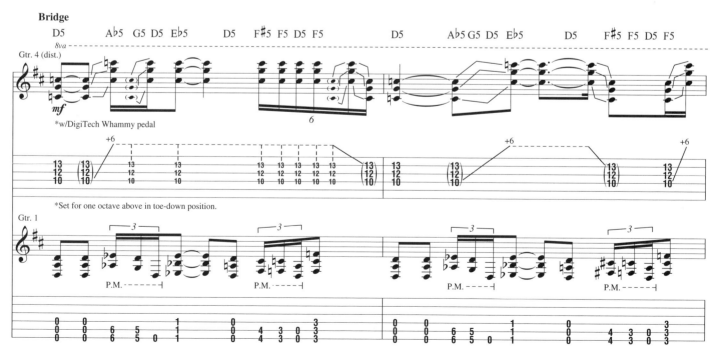

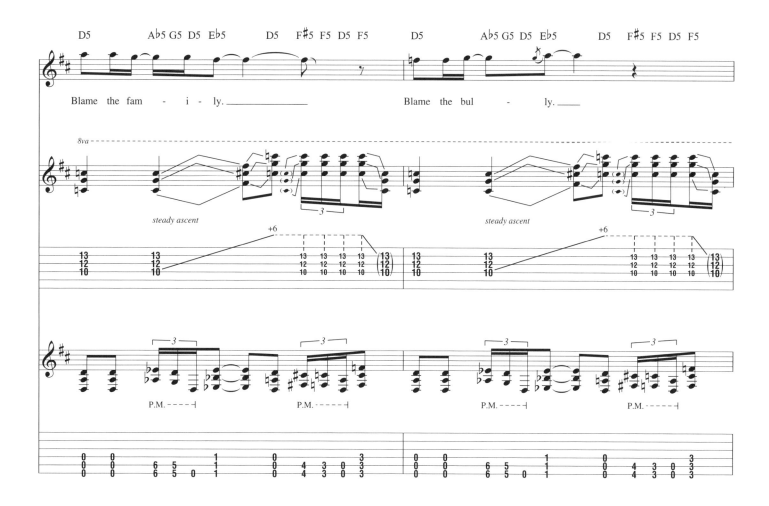

Blame the fam - i - ly. _____ Blame the bul - ly. _____

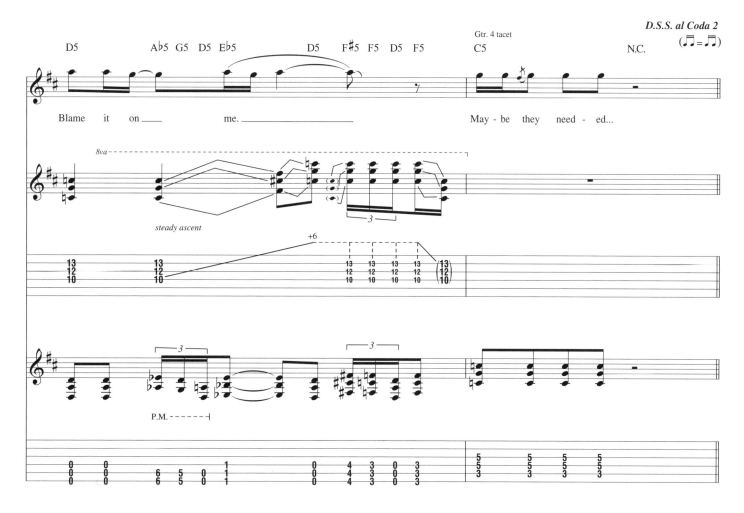

D.S.S. al Coda 2

Blame it on ____ me. _____ May - be they need - ed...

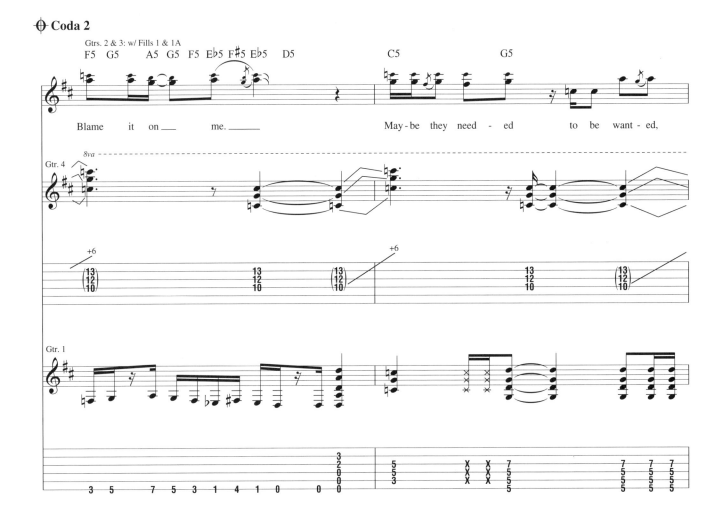

Blame it on ___ me. _____ May-be they need - ed to be want - ed,

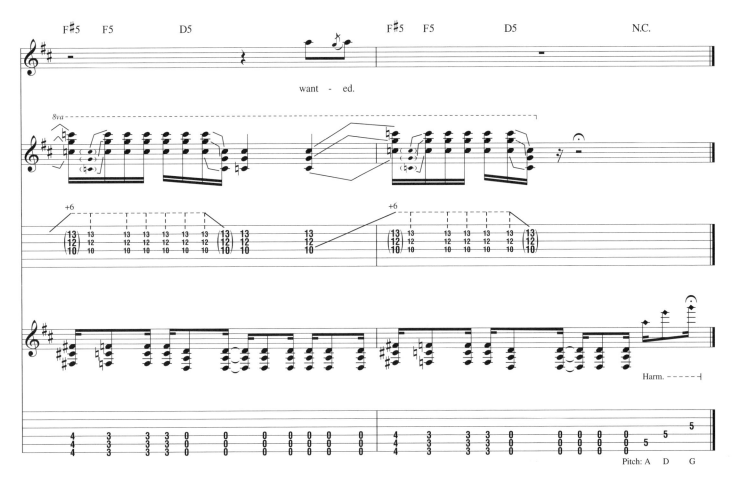

want - ed.

Drive By

Words and Music by Pat Monahan, Espen Lind and Amund Bjorklund

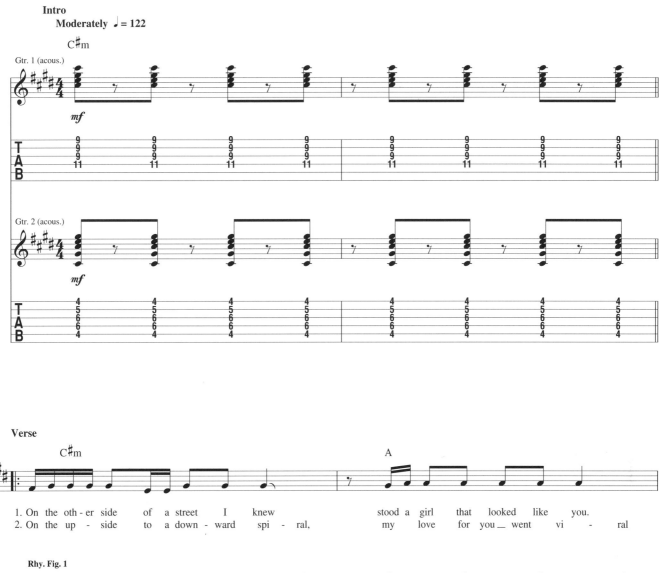

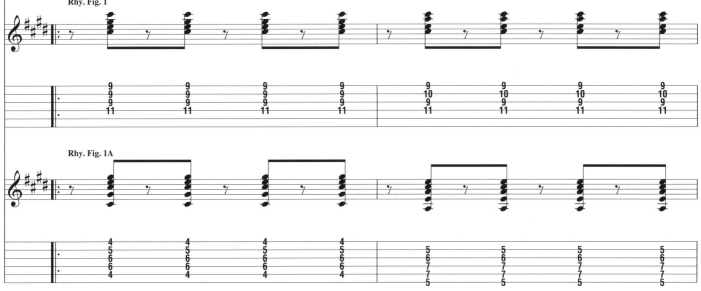

Verse lyrics:

1. On the oth-er side of a street I knew stood a girl that looked like you.
2. On the up-side to a down-ward spi-ral, my love for you _ went vi - ral

*Chord symbols reflect overall harmony.

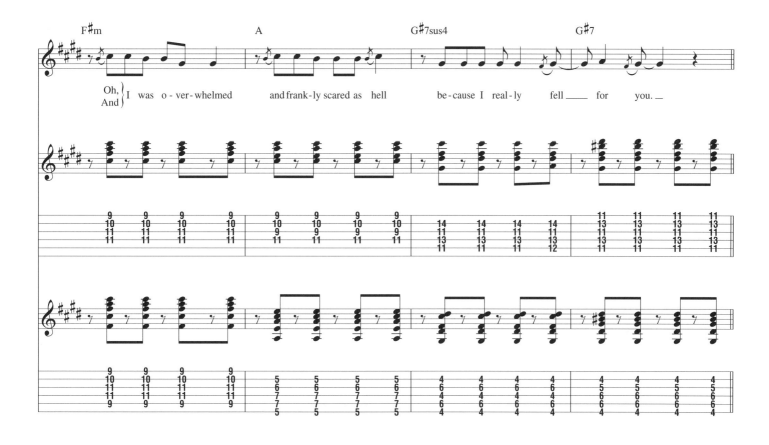

Oh,
And } I was o-ver-whelmed and frank-ly scared as hell be-cause I real-ly fell ___ for you. ___

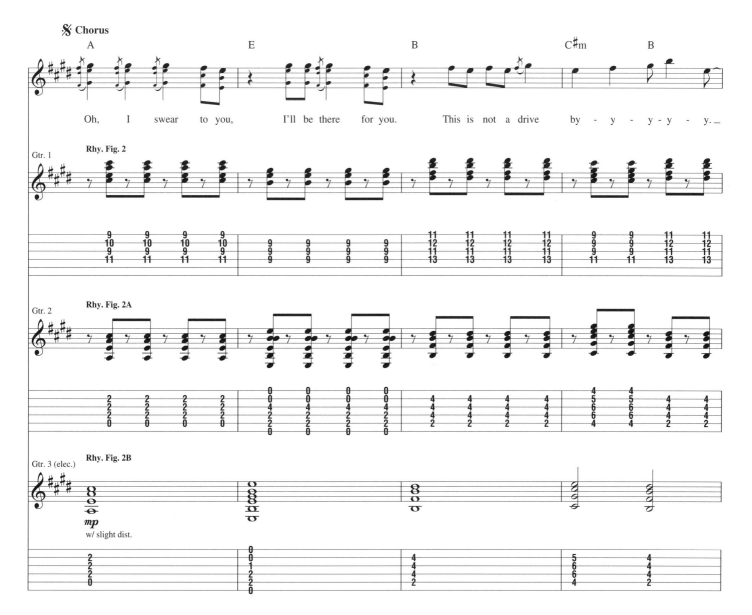

Chorus

Oh, I swear to you, I'll be there for you. This is not a drive by - y - y-y-y. ___

Just a shy guy, look-ing for a two ply Hef-ty bag to hold my - y-y-y-y-y-y love.

End Rhy. Fig. 2

End Rhy. Fig. 2A

End Rhy. Fig. 2B

Gtrs. 1, 2 & 3: w/ Rhy. Figs. 2, 2A & 2B

When you move me, ev - 'ry-thing is groov - y. They don't like it, sue me.

Mm, the way you do me. Oh, I swear to you, I'll be there for you.

there's noth - in' up my sleeve but love for you

ah.)

ah.)

ah,

Verse

Gtr. 3 tacet

3. On the oth-er side of a street I knew stood a girl that looked like you.

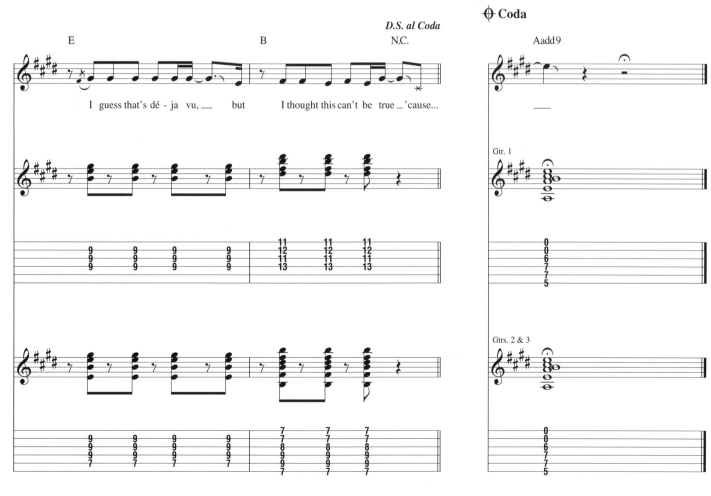

D.S. al Coda

I guess that's dé-ja vu, ___ but I thought this can't be true ___ 'cause...

✛ **Coda**

from **Family of the Year** - *Lomo Vista*
Hero
Words and Music by Joe Keefe

Capo V

Intro
Fast ♩ = 174

*F
(C)

Gtrs. 1 & 2
(acous.)

mf
w/ fingers
let ring throughout

*Symbols in parentheses represent chord names respective to capoed guitar.
Symbols above reflect actual sounding chords. Capoed fret is "0" in tab.

Chorus
F
(C)

Let _____ me go. _____ I don't wan - na be your _____

Riff A

Gtr. 1

Gtr. 2

*Composite arrangement

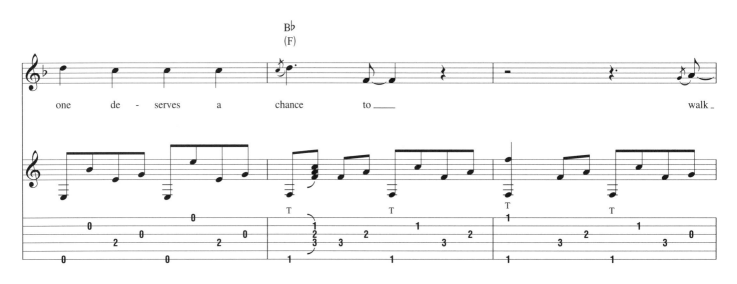

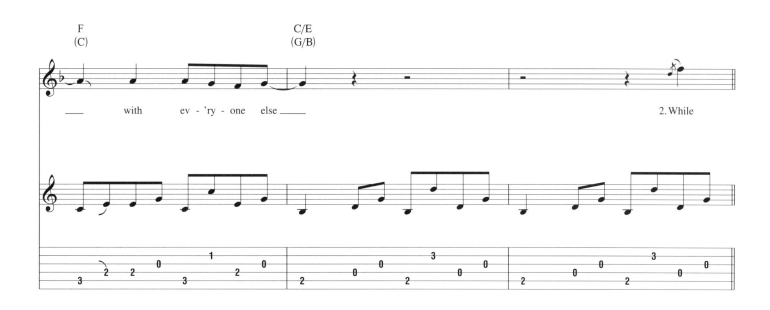

with ev - 'ry - one else _____   2. While

Verse

Gtrs. 1 & 2: w/ Riff A (1st 12 meas.)

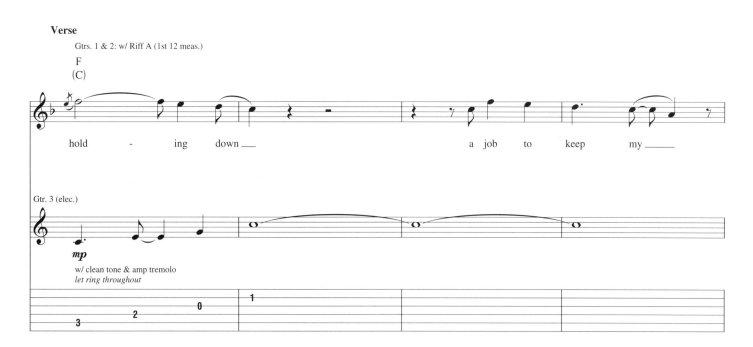

hold - ing down _____   a job to keep my _____

Gtr. 3 (elec.)

mp

w/ clean tone & amp tremolo
let ring throughout

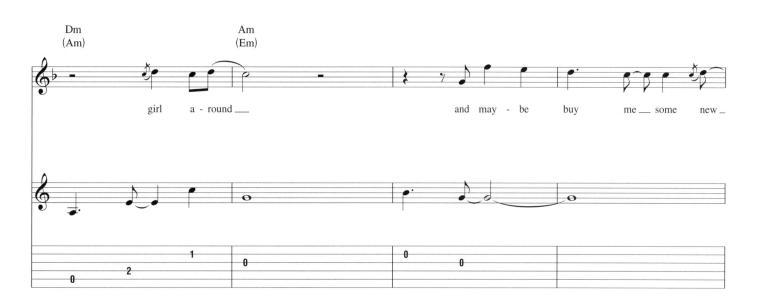

girl a - round _____   and may - be buy me ___ some new ___

strings   and her   a   night   out   on   the week - end.

3. And we can whis -

Gtr. 3

Riff B   **End Riff B**

Gtr. 1

Gtr. 2

Verse

Gtrs. 1 & 2: w/ Riff A (1st 8 meas.)

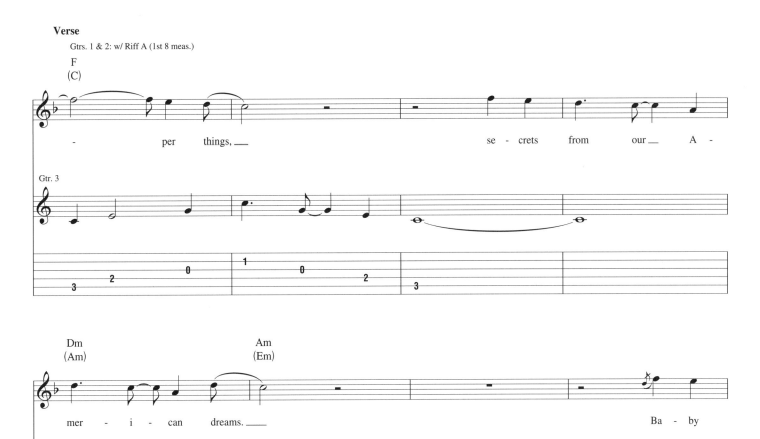

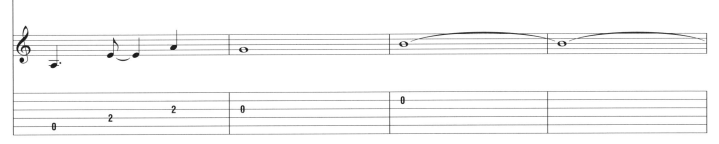

*Composite arrangement

Chorus

Gtrs. 1 & 2: w/ Riff A (1st 7 meas.)

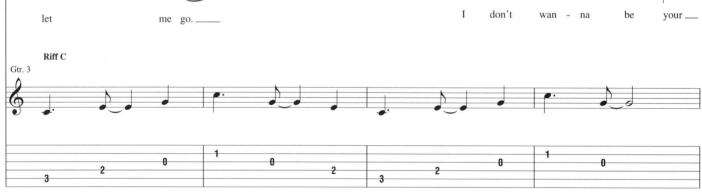

let   me go. ___   I don't wan - na be your ___

Riff C

Gtr. 3

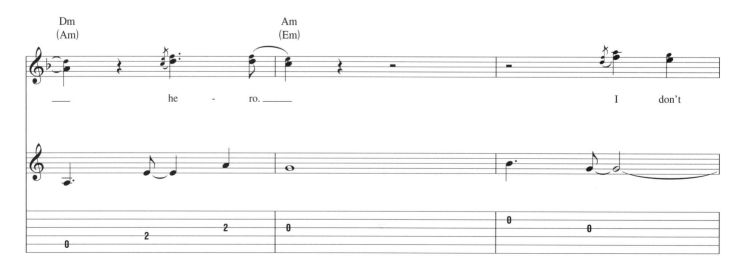

___ he - ro. ___   I don't

End Riff C

with ev - 'ry - one else.

Interlude

Gtrs. 1 & 2: w/ Riffs A & A1 (1st 8 meas.)

F
(C)

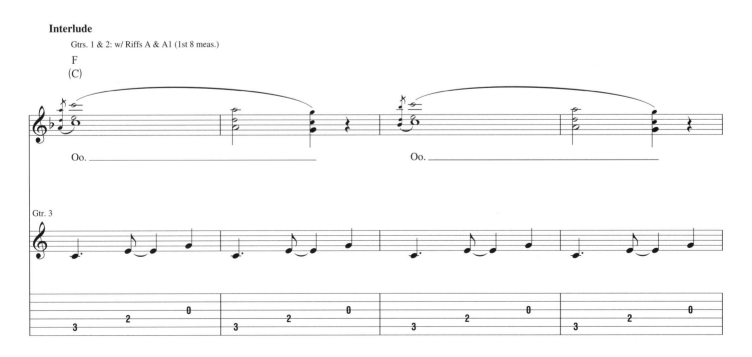

Oo. _____ Oo. _____

Gtr. 3

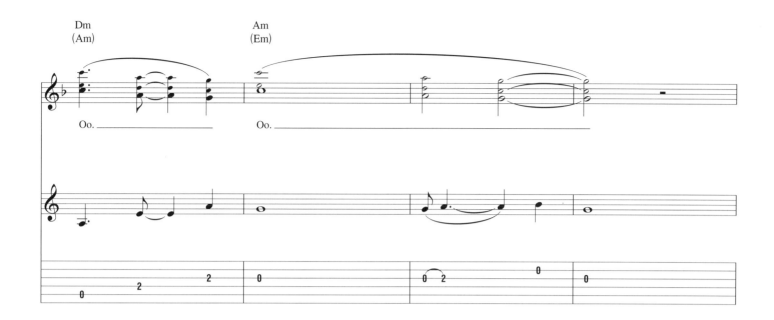

*Composite arrangement

Chorus

Gtrs. 1 & 2: w/ Riff A (1st 10 meas.)
Gtr. 3: w/ Riff C, simile
Gtr. 4 tacet

let   me go. ____   I don't wan - na be your

Rhy. Fig. 1

Gtr. 5 (elec.)

mf

*w/ slight dist. & delay

*Set for half-note regeneration w/ 2 repeats.

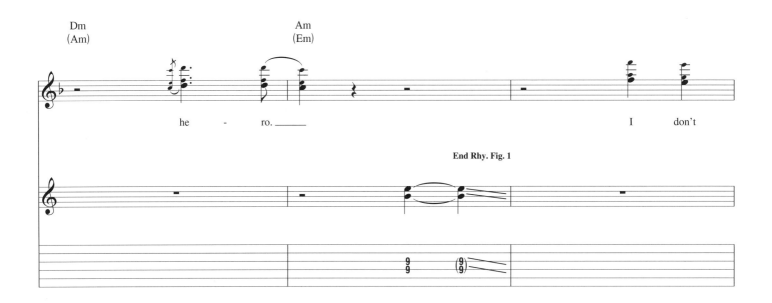

Verse

Gtrs. 1 & 2: w/ Riff A   Gtr. 5: w/ Rhy. Fig. 1
Gtr. 3: w/ Riff C (1st 4 meas.)

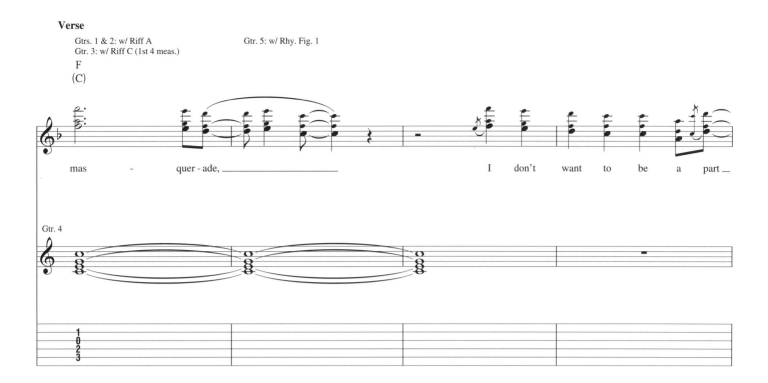

mas - quer - ade, _____   I don't want to be a part _____

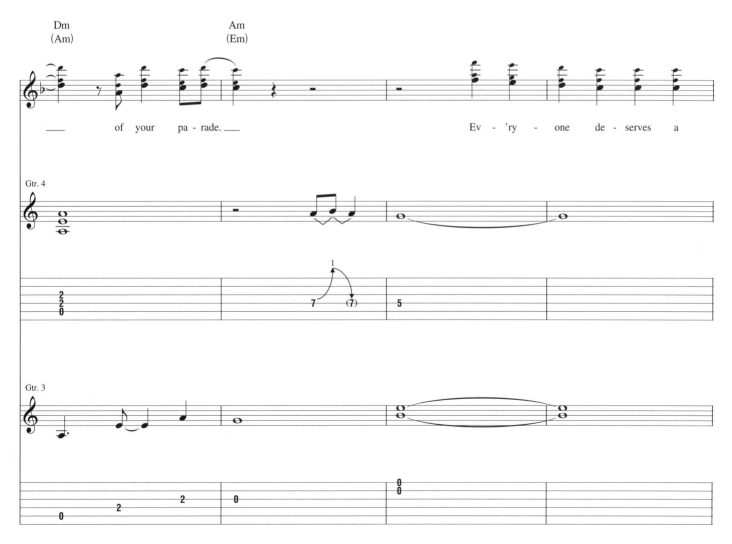

_____ of your pa - rade. _____   Ev - 'ry - one de - serves a

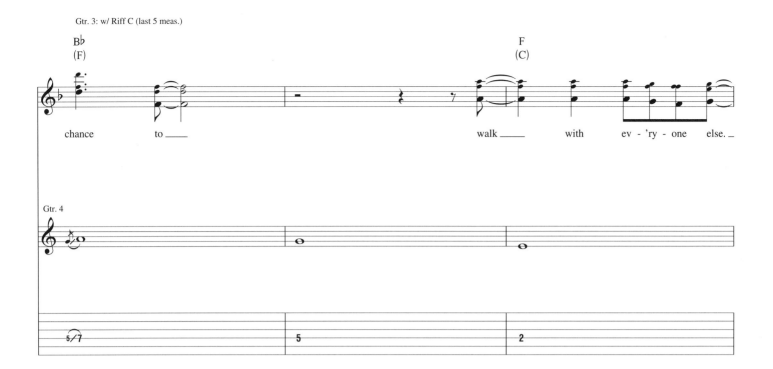

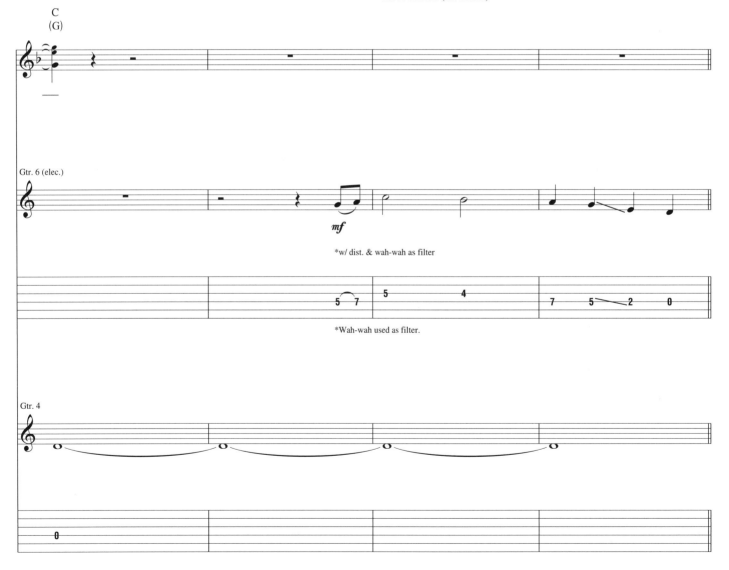

Outro

Gtrs. 1 & 2: w/ Riff A (1st 10 meas.)

F
(C)

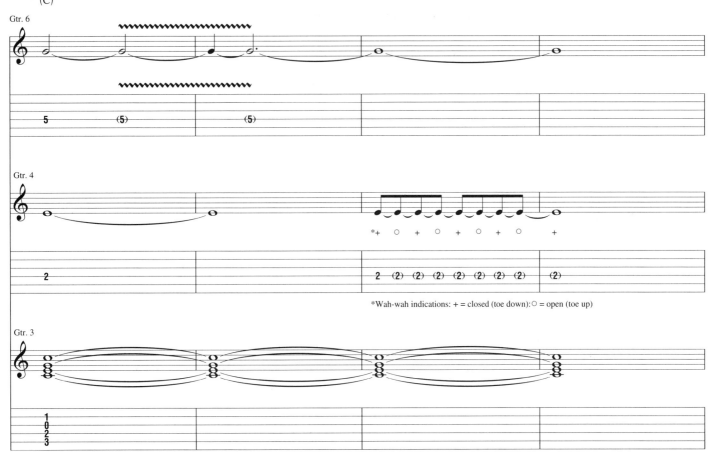

*Wah-wah indications: + = closed (toe down):○ = open (toe up)

Gtrs. 3, 4 & 6 tacet

Dm   Am   B♭
(Am)   (Em)   (F)

Ho Hey

Words and Music by Jeremy Fraites and Wesley Schultz

Double-time feel

End double-time feel

*See top of first page of song for chord diagrams pertaining to rhythm slashes.

**To play mandolin parts on guitar, capo 12th fret and tune highest four strings as follows: (low to high) G♯ -D♯ -A-E.

Interlude

Bkgd. Voc.: w/ Voc. Fig. 1 (4 times)
Gtr. 1: w/ Rhy. Fig. 1 (2 times)

Verse

Bkgd. Voc.: w/ Voc. Fig. 1 (4 times)
Mandolin: w/ Rhy. Fig. 4
Gtr. 1: w/ Rhy. Fig. 1

Gtr. 1: w/ Rhy. Fig. 2

Home

Words and Music by Greg Holden and Drew Pearson

*Bass plays B.

**Bass plays A.

*Two gtrs. arr. for one.

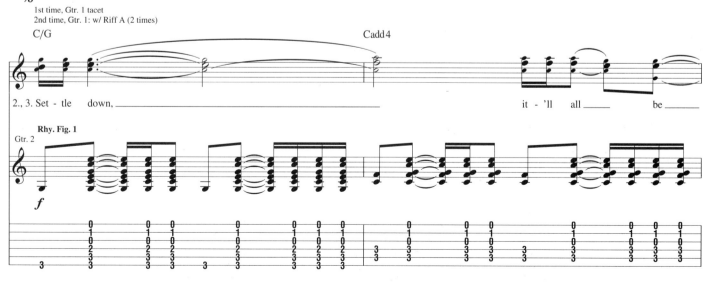

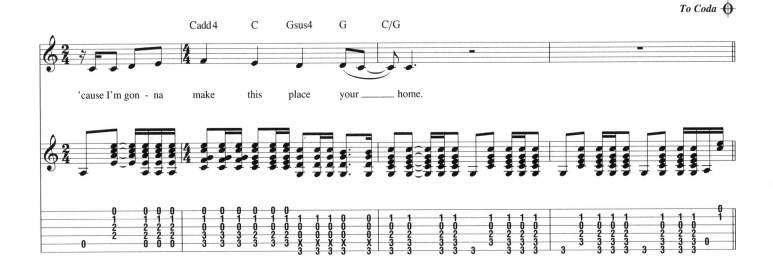

Cadd4   C   Gsus4   G   C/G

'cause I'm gon - na   make   this   place   your _____ home.

Chorus

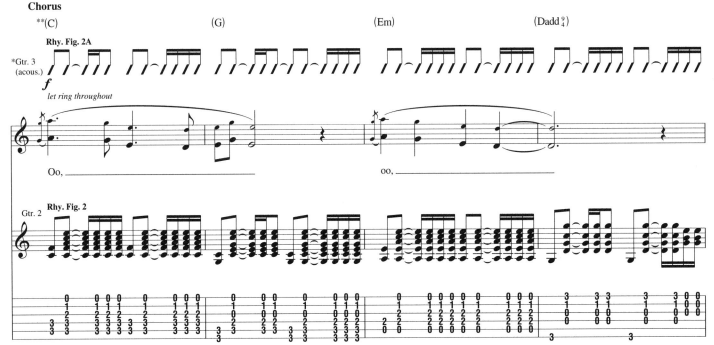

**(C)   (G)   (Em)   (Dadd $\frac{9}{4}$)

Rhy. Fig. 2A

*Gtr. 3
(acous.)

f

let ring throughout

Oo, _____   oo, _____

Gtr. 2   Rhy. Fig. 2

*Two gtrs. arr. for one.

**Symbols in parentheses represent chord names respective to capoed guitar.
See top of first page for chord diagrams pertaining to rhythm slashes.

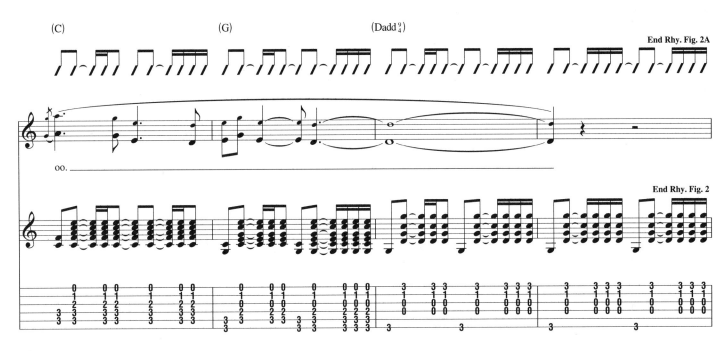

(C)   (G)   (Dadd $\frac{9}{4}$)

End Rhy. Fig. 2A

oo. _____

End Rhy. Fig. 2

*Symbols in parentheses represent chord names respective to capoed guitar.
Symbols above reflect actual sounding chords.

**Organ arr. for gtr.

from Imagine Dragons - *Night Visions*

It's Time

Words and Music by Daniel Reynolds, Benjamin McKee and Daniel Sermon

And now it's time to build __ from the bot-tom of __ the pit __ right to the top. __

End Riff B

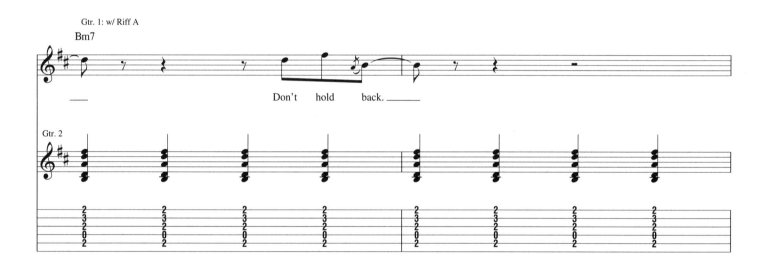

Gtr. 1: w/ Riff A

__ Don't hold back. _____

Gtr. 2

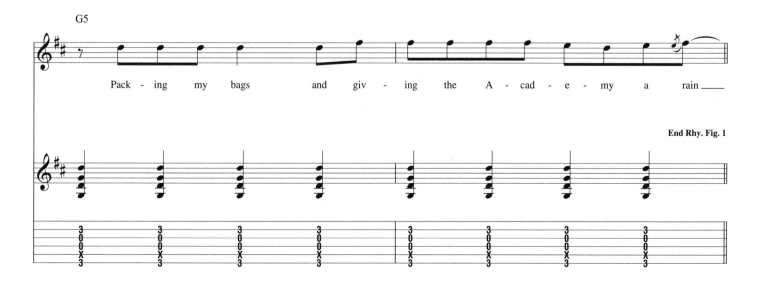

Pack - ing my bags and giv - ing the A - cad - e - my a rain ____

End Rhy. Fig. 1

Pre-Chorus

Gtr. 1: w/ Riff B
Gtr. 2: w/ Rhy. Fig. 1

D5   Dsus2/A

___check.   I don't ev-er want to let you down. _   I don't ev-er want to leave this town. _

Gtr. 1: w/ Riff A

Bm7   G5

_____   'Cause, af - ter all, ____   this cit - y nev - er sleeps at night. _ It's

Chorus

D5   B5

time to be-gin, is - n't it?   I get a lit-tle bit big-ger, but then I'll ad-mit I'm just the same as I

Riff C

*Gtr. 3   *8va*

mf

22   21   17
           19

*Kybd. arr. for gtr.

Rhy. Fig. 2

**Gtrs. 4 & 5

mf

```
7 7 7 7 7 7 7 7 | 7 7 7 7 7 7 7 0 | 4 4 4 4 4 4 4 4 | 4 4 4 4 4 4 4 4
5 5 5 5 5 5 5 5 | 5 5 5 5 5 5 5 0 | 2 2 2 2 2 2 2 2 | 2 2 2 2 2 2 2 2
```

**Gtr. 4 (acous.); Gtr. 5 (elec.) w/ clean tone
Composite arrangement

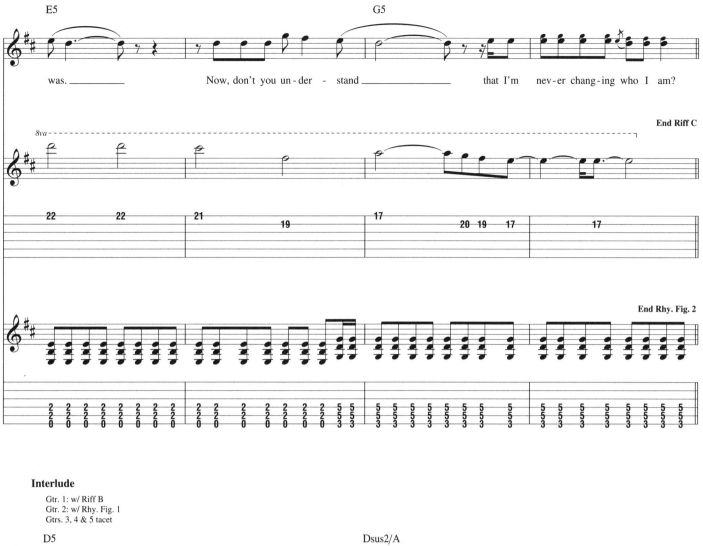

was. _____ Now, don't you un - der - stand _____ that I'm nev - er chang - ing who I am?

End Riff C

End Rhy. Fig. 2

Interlude

Gtr. 1: w/ Riff B
Gtr. 2: w/ Rhy. Fig. 1
Gtrs. 3, 4 & 5 tacet

D5   Dsus2/A

Gtr. 1: w/ Riff A

Bm7   G5

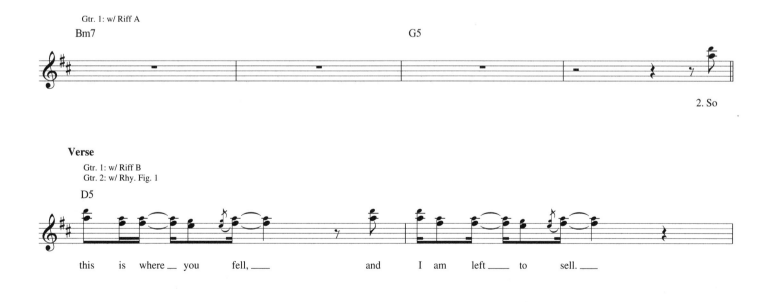

2. So

Verse

Gtr. 1: w/ Riff B
Gtr. 2: w/ Rhy. Fig. 1

D5

this   is   where __ you   fell, ___   and   I   am   left __ to   sell. ___

Dsus2/A

The   path   to   heav - en   runs __ through   miles   of   cloud - ed   hell, __   right   to   the   top. __

Bridge

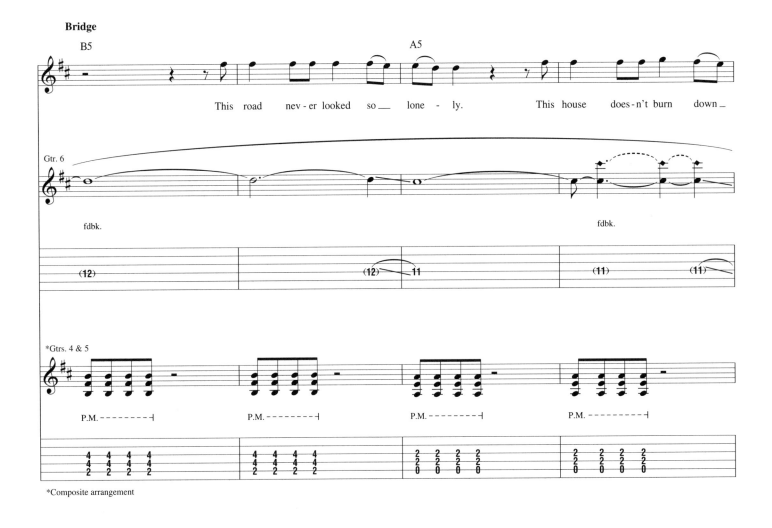

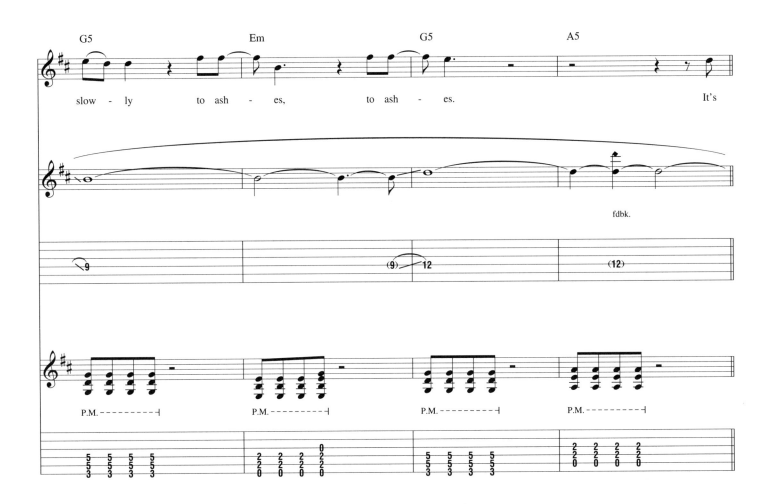

Chorus

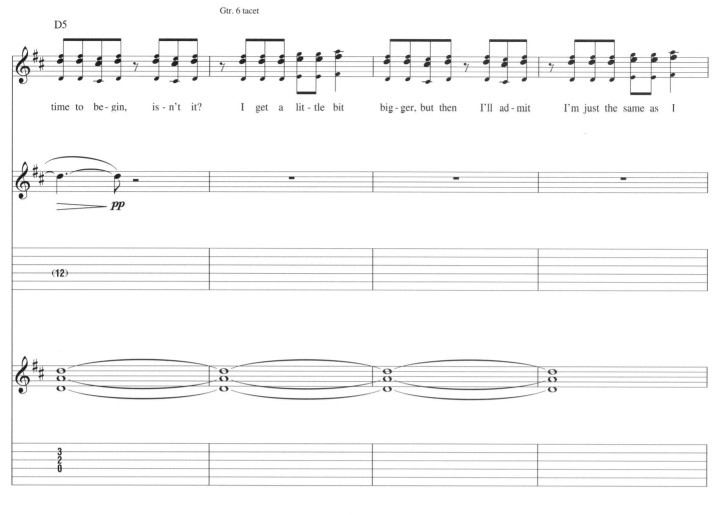

time to be - gin, is - n't it? I get a lit - tle bit big - ger, but then I'll ad - mit I'm just the same as I

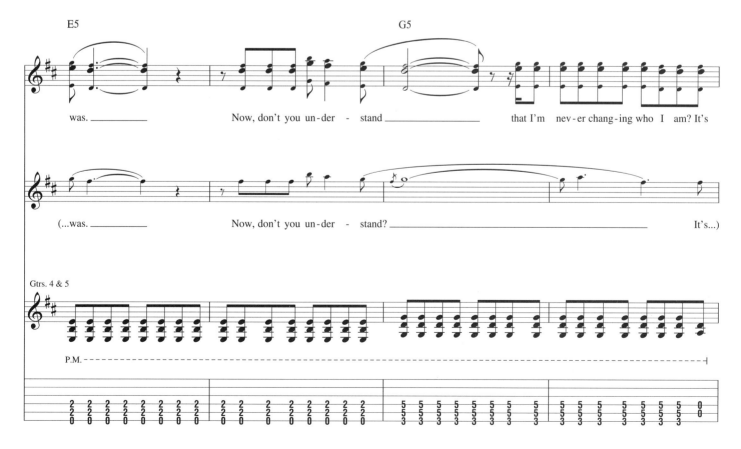

was. _____ Now, don't you un - der - stand _____ that I'm nev - er chang - ing who I am? It's

(...was. _____ Now, don't you un - der - stand? _____ It's...)

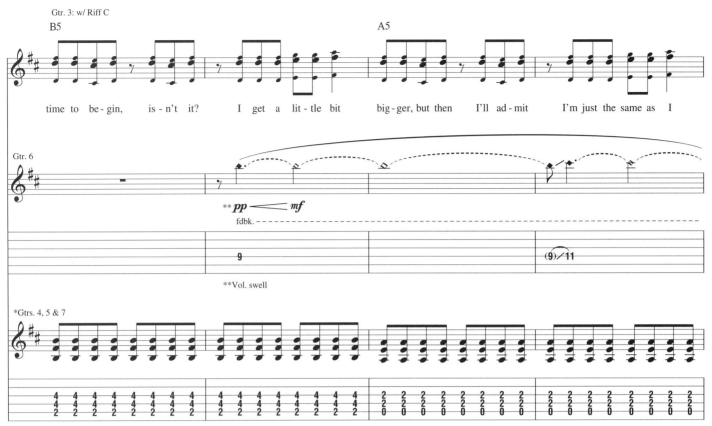

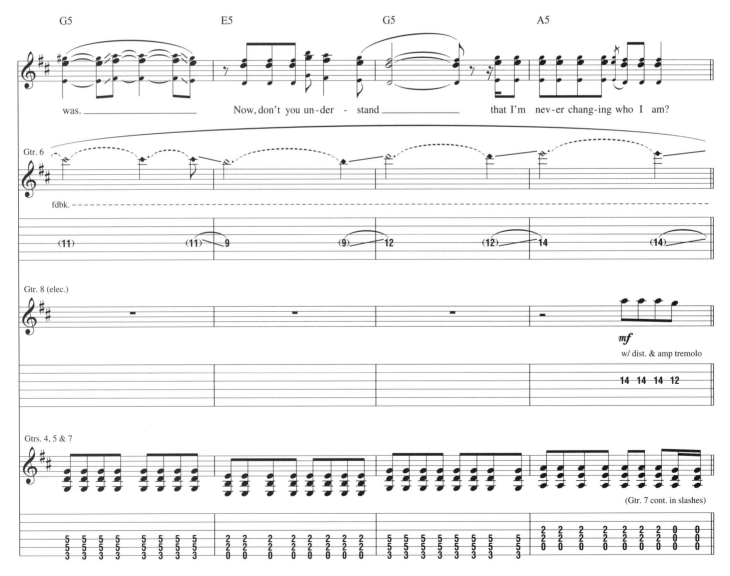

Outro

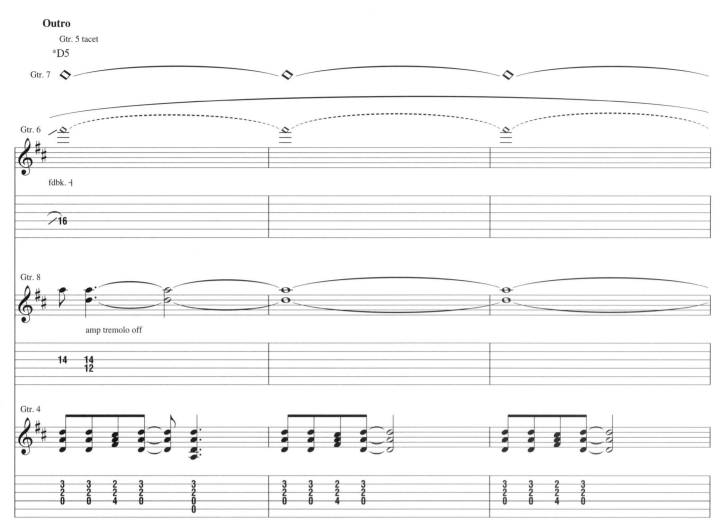

*See top of first page of song for chord diagrams pertaining to rhythm slashes.

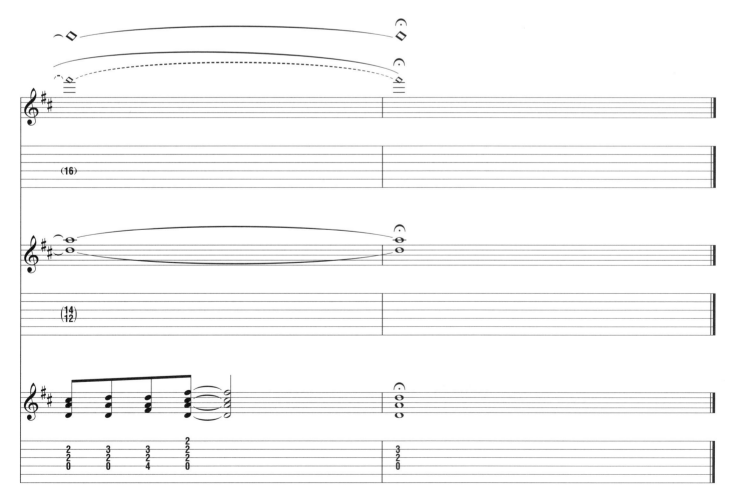

Little Talks

Words and Music by Nanna Hilmarsdottir and Ragnar Thorhallsson

Capo I

Intro
Very fast ♩ = 205

*Horn section arr. for gtr.

**Gtrs. 2 & 3 (elec.) w/ clean tone;
Gtr. 4 (acous.). Composite arrangement

***Symbols in parentheses represent chord names respective to capoed guitar.
Symbols above reflect actual sounding chords. Capoed fret is "0" in tab.

†Gang vocals, next 9 meas.

Gtrs. 2, 3 & 4: w/ Rhy. Fig. 1 (3 times)
Gtr. 5: w/ Rhy. Fig. 1A (3 times)

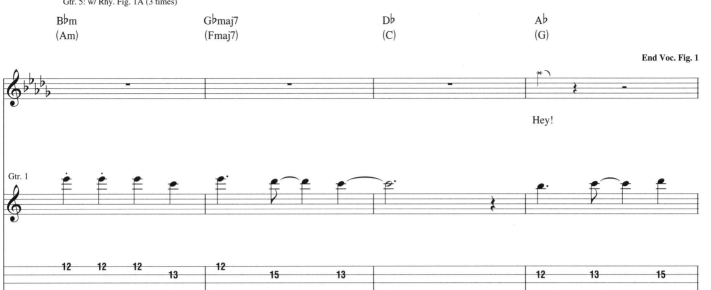

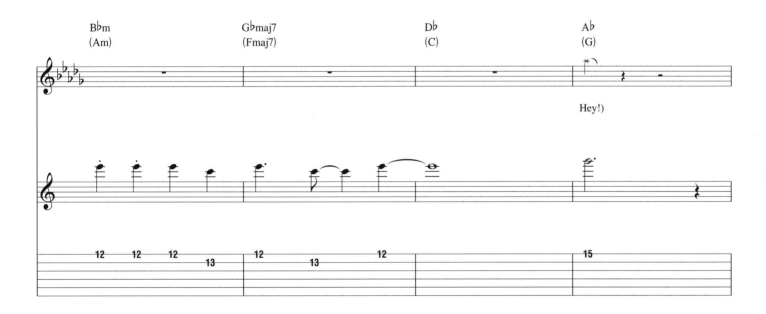

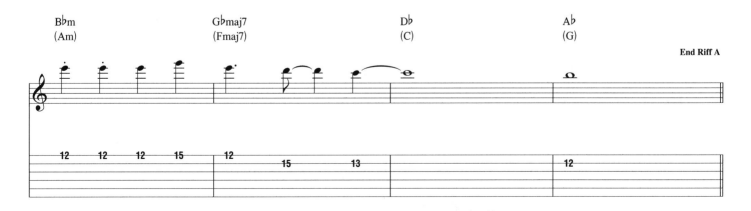

71

𝄋 Verse

2nd time, Gtrs. 2, 3 & 4: w/ Rhy. Fig. 3 (6 times)

Gtrs. 1, 3, 4 & 5 tacet

2nd time, Gtr. 5: w/ Rhy. Fig. 3A (6 times)

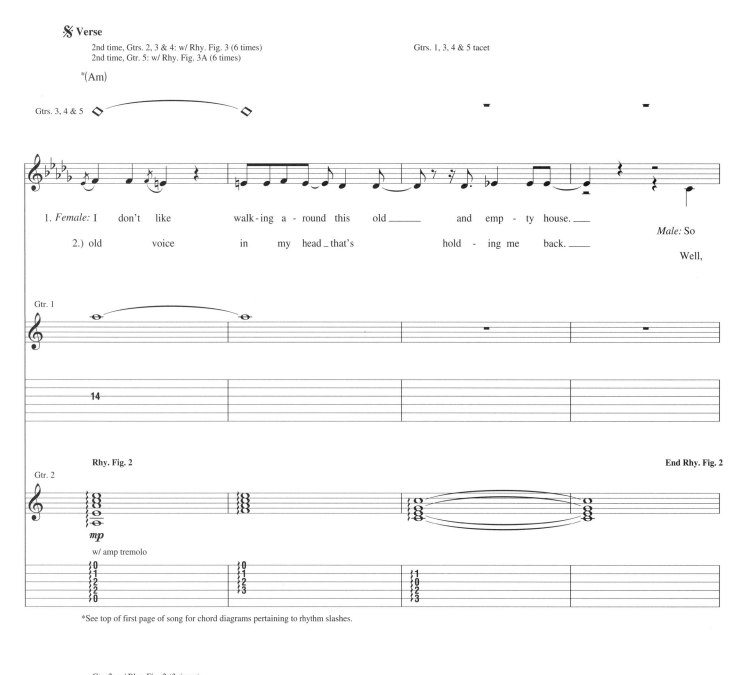

1. *Female:* I don't like walk-ing a - round this old _____ and emp - ty house. _____

2.) old voice in my head __ that's hold - ing me back. _____

Male: So

Well,

*See top of first page of song for chord diagrams pertaining to rhythm slashes.

Gtr. 2: w/ Rhy. Fig. 2 (3 times)

| B♭m | G♭maj7 | D♭ |
| (Am) | (Fmaj7) | (C) |

hold my hand, I'll walk with you, __ my dear. _____

tell her that I miss our lit - tle talks. _____

The

| B♭m | G♭maj7 | D♭ |
| (Am) | (Fmaj7) | (C) |

stairs creek as you sleep, __ it's keep - ing me a - wake. _____

Soon it will be o - ver _____ and bur - ied with our _____ past.

It's the

We

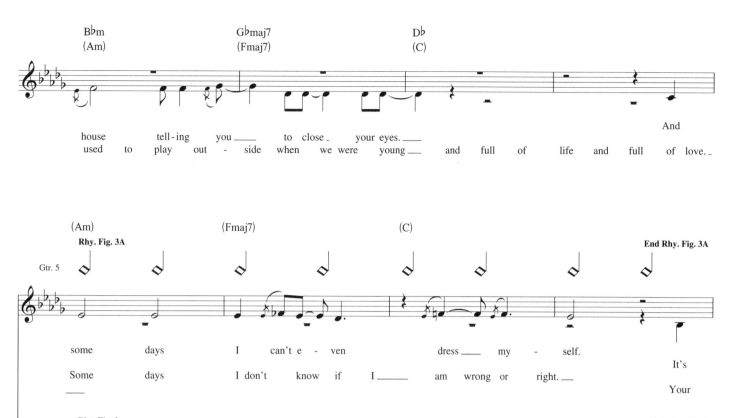

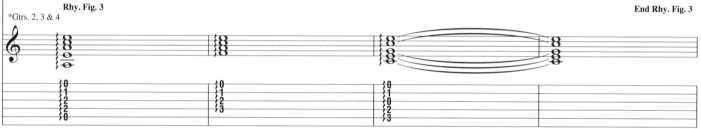

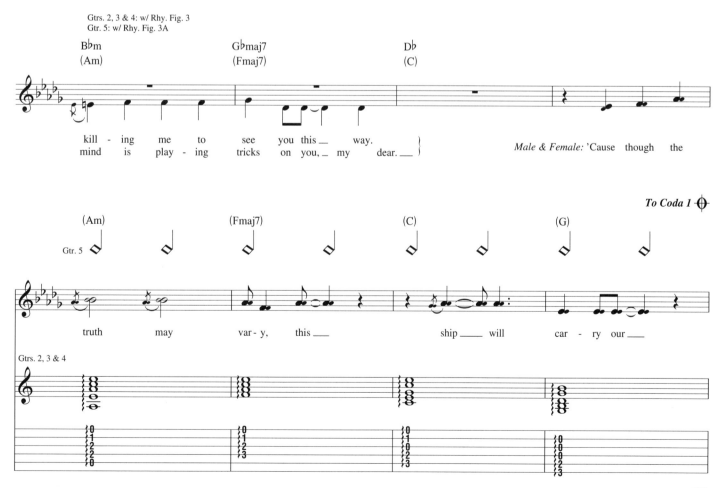

(Yelled: Hey!)

Hey!

Hey!)

2. *Female:* There's an

⊕ Coda 1

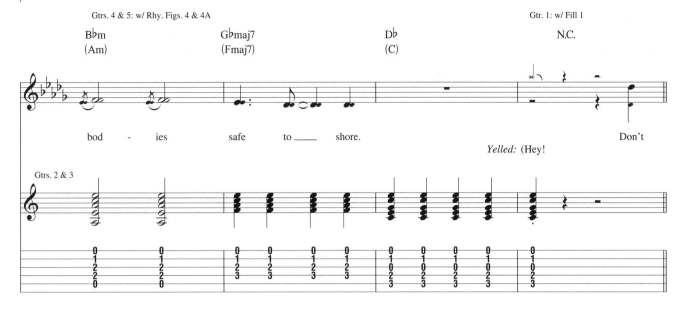

𝄋𝄋 Chorus

1st & 2nd time, Bkgd. Voc.: w/ Voc. Fig. 1
1st time, Gtrs. 2, 3 & 4: w/ Rhy. Fig. 1 (4 times)
1st time, Gtr. 5: w/ Rhy. Fig. 1A (4 times)
2nd time, Gtrs. 2, 3 & 4: w/ Rhy. Fig. 1 (7 times)
2nd time, Gtr. 5: w/ Rhy. Fig. 1A (7 times)

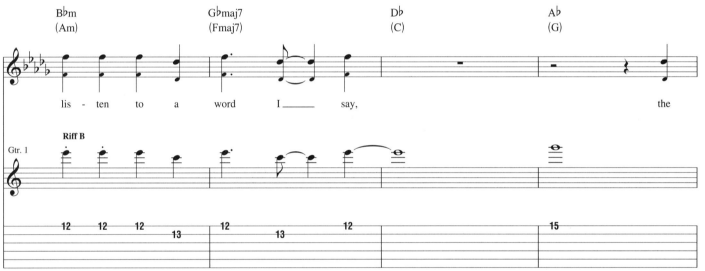

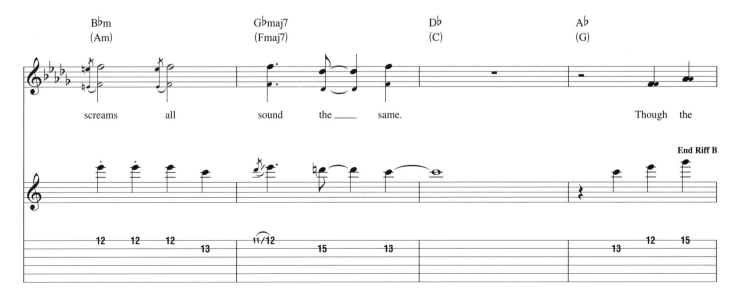

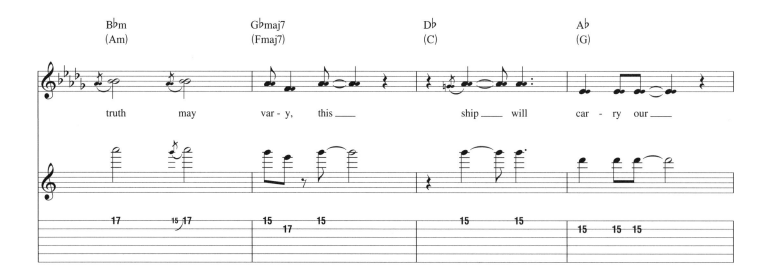

truth may var - y, this ___ ship ___ will car - ry our ___

To Coda 2

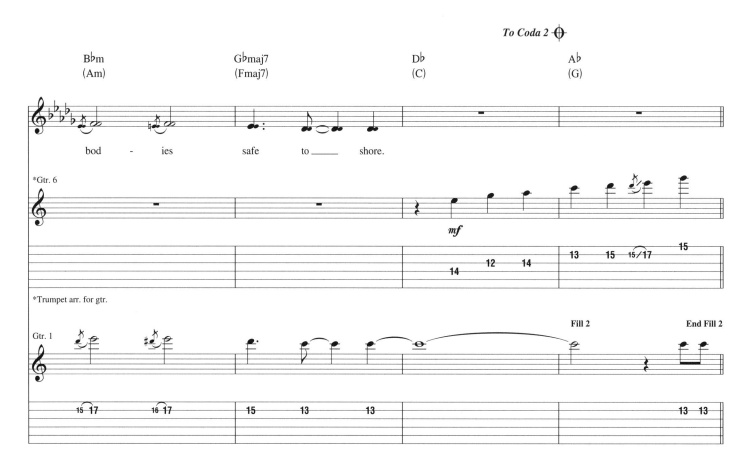

bod - ies safe to ___ shore.

*Gtr. 6

*Trumpet arr. for gtr.

Gtr. 1

Fill 2   End Fill 2

Interlude

Gtr. 1: w/ Riff B
Gtrs. 2, 3 & 4: w/ Rhy. Fig. 1 (3 times)
Gtr. 5: w/ Rhy. Fig. 1A (3 times)

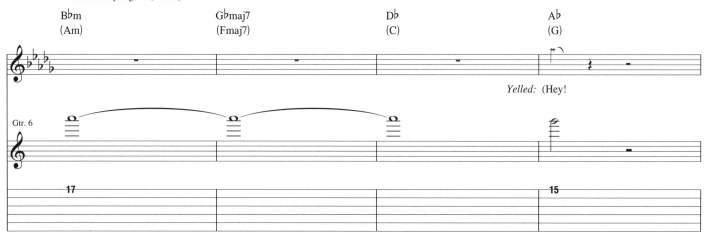

Yelled: (Hey!

Gtr. 6

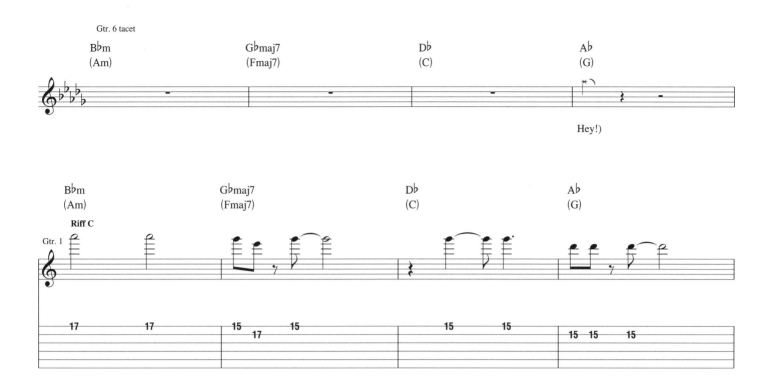

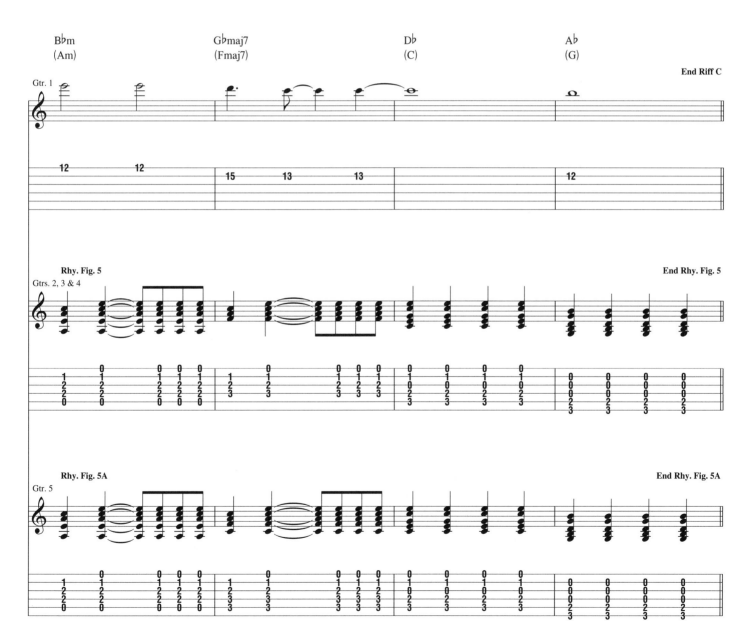

Interlude

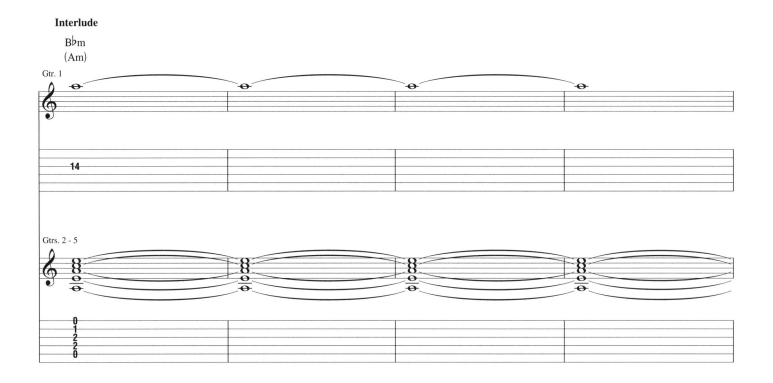

Verse

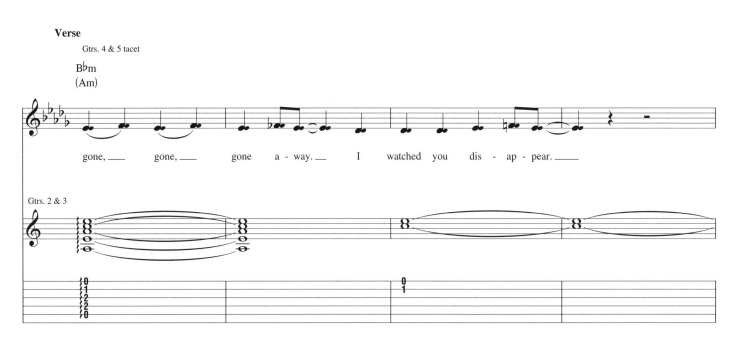

gone, ___ gone, ___ gone a - way. ___ I watched you dis - ap - pear. ___

3. You're

from Bruno Mars - *Unorthodox Jukebox*

Locked Out of Heaven

Words and Music by Bruno Mars, Ari Levine and Philip Lawrence

*See top of first page of song for chord diagrams pertaining to rhythm slashes.

**w/ echo set for half-note regeneration w/ 1 repeat where indicated, next 16 meas.

***long   †long

Coda

C5   N.C.

*lo,   oo,   ah,   oo,   ooh,   ah, _____   ong. _____

Gtr. 2

Gtr. 1

*long

Bridge

Gtr. 1: w/ Rhy. Fig. 2 (2 times)
Gtr. 2: w/ Riff A (2 times)

B♭5   G5

Oh,   oo, whoa,   oo, whoa,   oo, whoa.   Yeah,   ee, yeah,   ee, yeah.   Can I just

F5   C5   1.   2.

stay   here, _   spend the rest of my   days _ here? _____   _ 'Cause you make me

Chorus

Gtr. 2: w/ Riff B (1 3/4 times)

B♭5   G5

feel _____ like _____   I've been locked out-ta heav - en _____   for too

**w/ echo as before

F5   C5

***lo,   oo, ah, oo, ong,   for too †lo, oo, ah, oo, ah,   ong. _____ Yeah, you make me

***long   †long

Oh Love

Words and Music by Billie Joe Armstrong, Mike Dirnt and Tre Cool

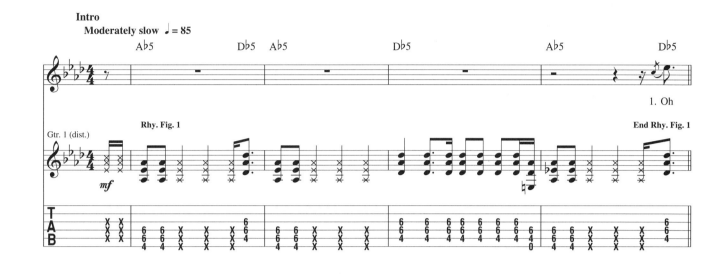

love, ____   oh   love, ____   won't   you   rain   on __ me   to - night? _____   Oh

life, ____   oh   life, _____   please   don't   pass   me   by. _____   Don't

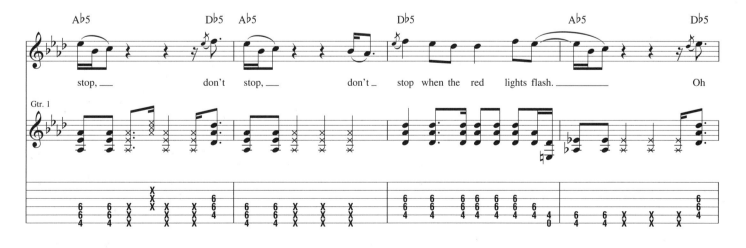

stop, ____   don't   stop, ____   don't   stop   when   the   red   lights   flash. _____   Oh

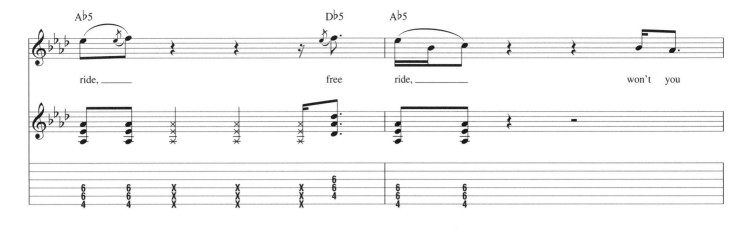

ride, _____ free ride, _____ won't you

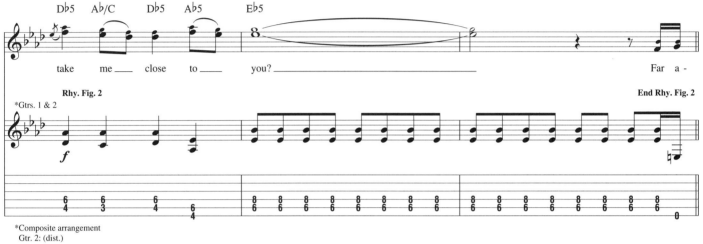

take me ___ close to ___ you? _____ Far a-

*Composite arrangement
Gtr. 2: (dist.)

Chorus

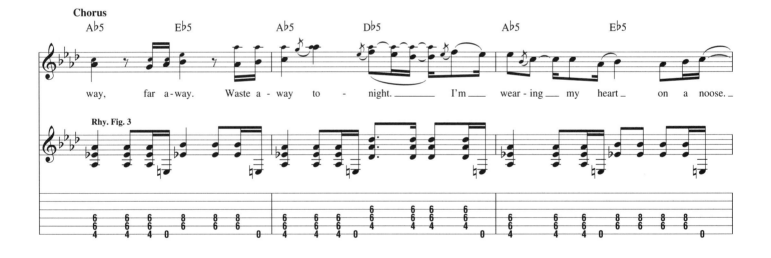

way, far a-way. Waste a-way to - night. _____ I'm ___ wear-ing ___ my heart ___ on a noose. ___

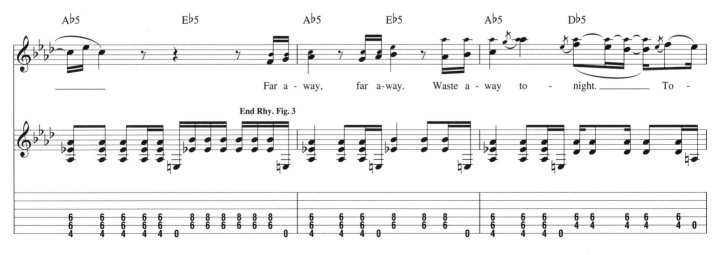

_____ Far a-way, far a-way. Waste a-way to - night. _____ To -

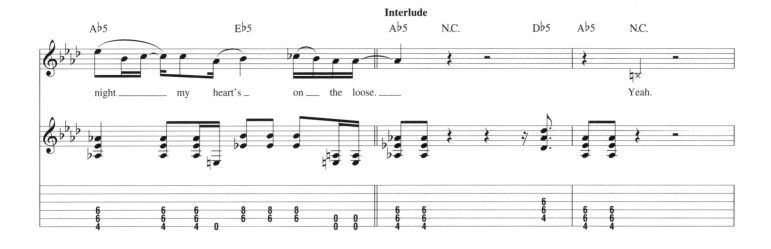

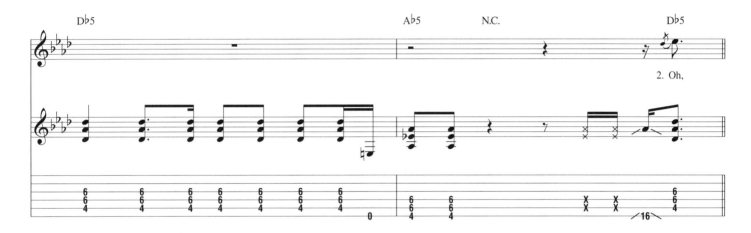

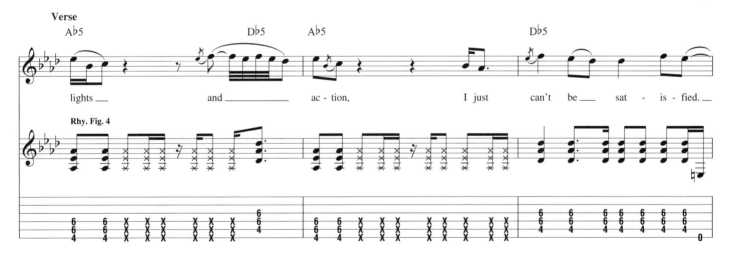

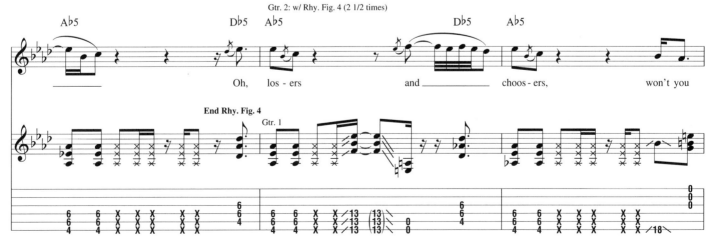

Bridge

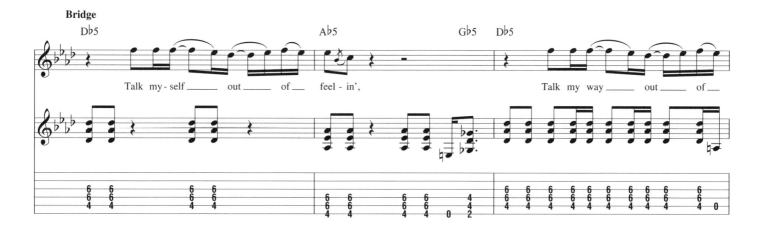

Talk my-self ___ out ___ of ___ feel-in', Talk my way ___ out ___ of ___

con - trol. Talk my-self ___ out ___ of ___ fall - in' ___ in love,

P.M.

fall in love _____ with ___ you. Yeah!

f

Gtr.4 (dist.)

Gtrs. 1 & 2

Guitar Solo

Gtrs. 1 & 2: w/ Rhy. Fig. 3 (1 1/2 times)

Gtr. 4

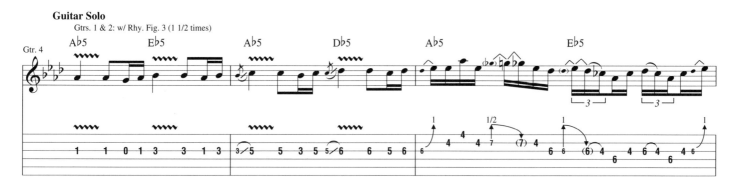

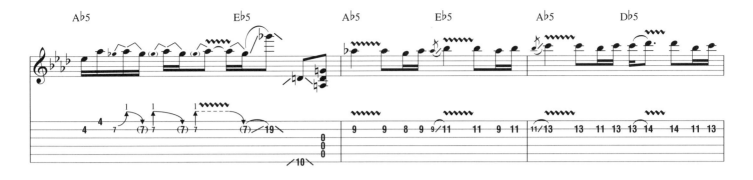

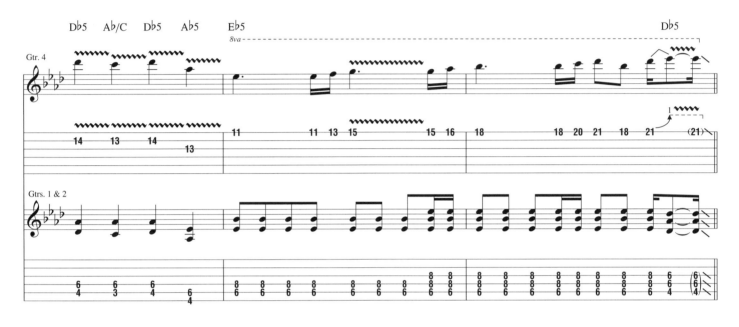

Interlude

Gtr. 1: w/ Rhy. Fig. 1
Gtrs. 2 & 4 tacet

3. Oh,

Verse

Gtr. 1: w/ Rhy. Fig. 1 (1 1/2 times)

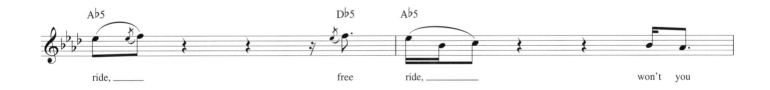

love, ___ oh love, ___ won't you rain on ___ me to-night? ___ Oh

ride, ___ free ride, ___ won't you

Gtrs. 1 & 2: w/ Rhy. Fig. 2

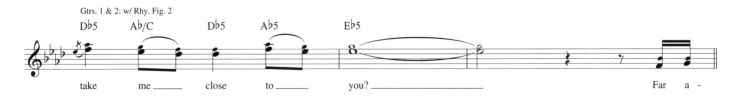

take me ___ close to ___ you? ___ Far a-

Chorus

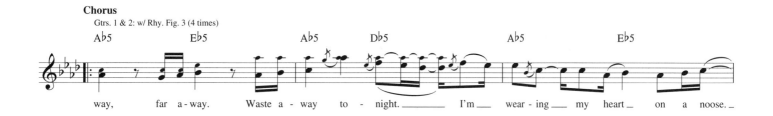

Gtrs. 1 & 2: w/ Rhy. Fig. 3 (4 times)

way, far a - way. Waste a - way to - night. _____ I'm ___ wear - ing ___ my heart ___ on a noose. _____

_____ Far a - way, far a - way. Waste a - way to - night. _____ To -

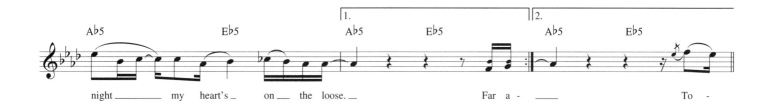

night _____ my heart's _ on ___ the loose. ___   Far a - _____   To -

Gtrs. 1 & 2: w/ Rhy. Fig. 3 (last 2 meas.)

night _____ my heart's _ on ___ the loose. ___   To -

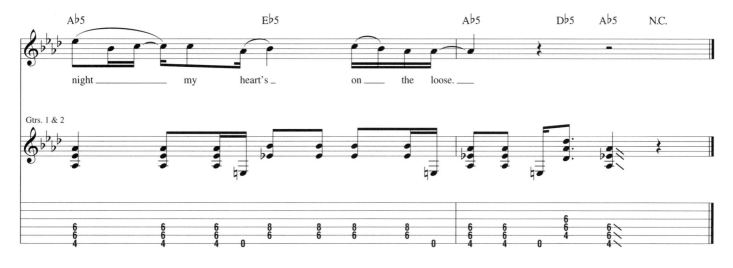

night _____ my heart's _ on ___ the loose. ___

Gtrs. 1 & 2

from Bon Iver - *For Emma, Forever Ago*
Skinny Love
Words and Music by Justin Vernon

Open C tuning:
(low to high) C-G-E-G-C-C

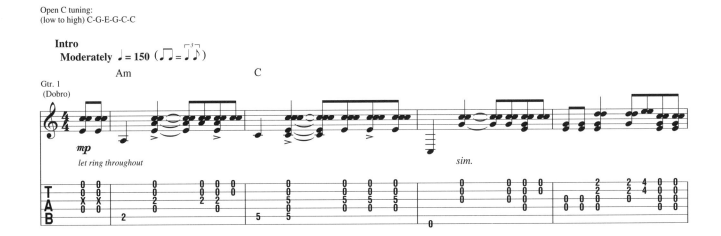

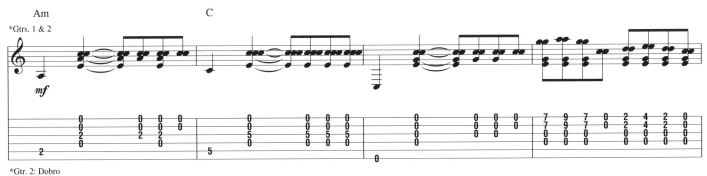

*Gtr. 2: Dobro
Composite arrangement

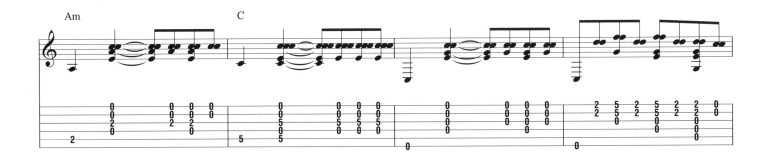

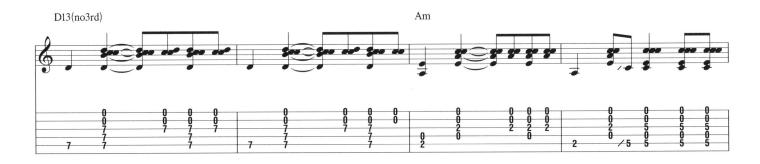

Verse

1. Come on, ____ skin-ny love, ____ just last the year.

*Vocals doubled throughout

Pour a lit-tle salt, ____ we were nev-er here. ____ My, my, my, _

____ my, my, my, ____ my, ____ my. Star-in' at the

sink ____ of blood __ and crushed ve-neer.

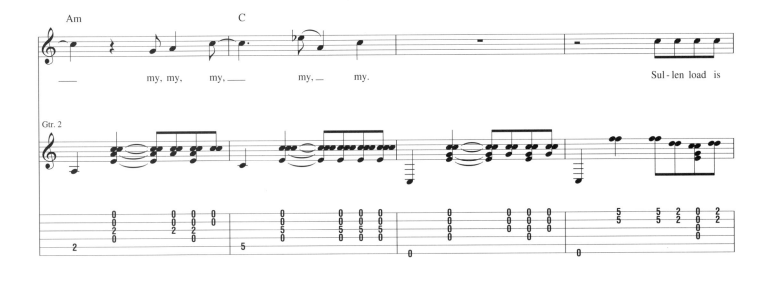

my, my, my, my, my. Sul - len load is

full, _____ so slow on _____ the split. _____

D.S. al Coda

And I've

☩ **Coda**

Who will love you? Who will fight? _

Who will fall _____ far be-

100

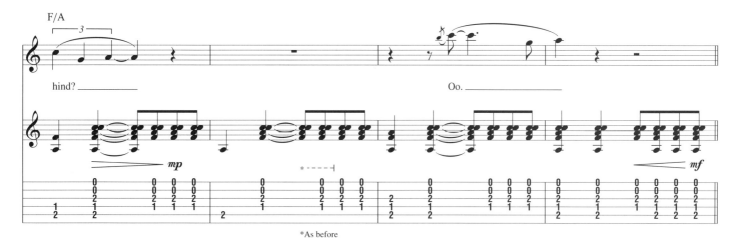

hind? _____ Oo. _____

*As before

Outro

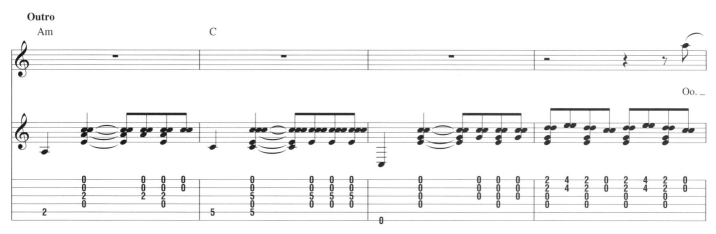

Oo. ___

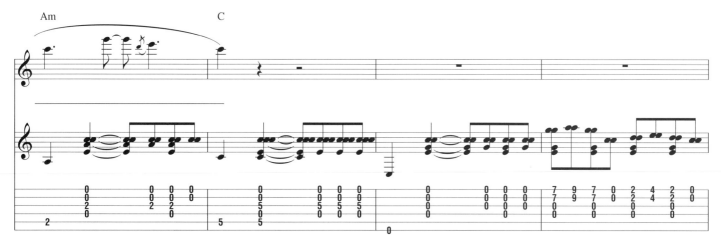

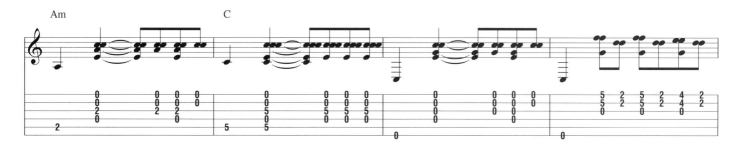

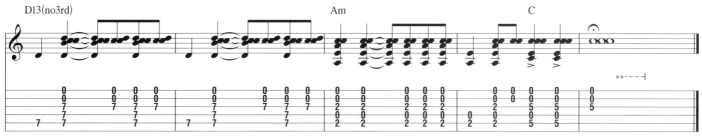

**As before

from Volbeat - *Beyond Hell/Above Heaven*

Still Counting

Words and Music by Jon Larsen, Thomas Bredahl, Anders Kjolholm and Michael Poulsen

Interlude

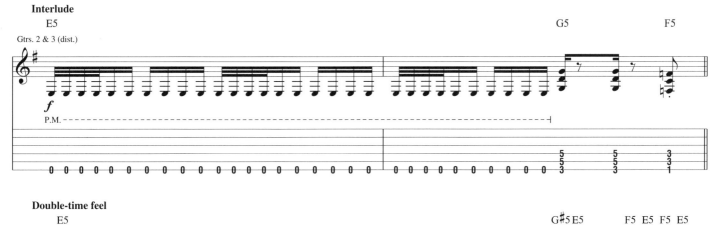

Double-time feel

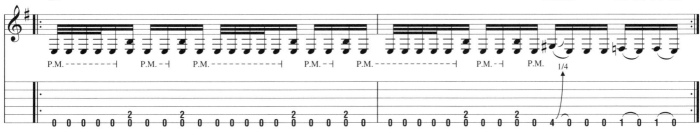

End double-time feel

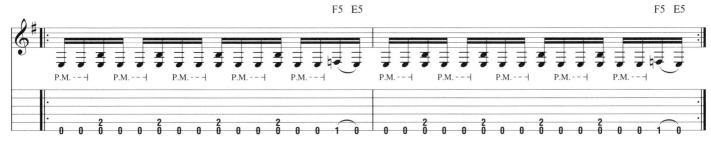

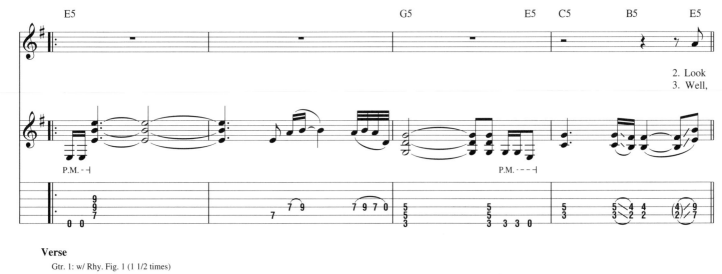

2. Look
3. Well,

Verse

Gtr. 1: w/ Rhy. Fig. 1 (1 1/2 times)

deep in-to your-self be-fore you   blame __   all oth-ers for be-tray - al,   now, for be-tray-
may-be you think __ your lie is   safe, __   but I read you like a let - ter.   You're like a let-

A prom-ise so eas-y to say, ____ and eas-y, you failed,
Your charms do not e-vince the pain, ____ it fills ____ me with rage ____

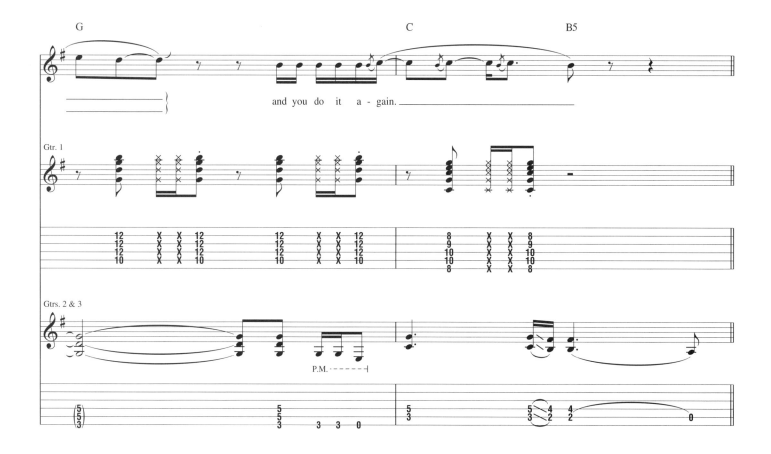

and you do it a-gain. ____

Chorus
Double-time feel

Gtr. 1 tacet

C5

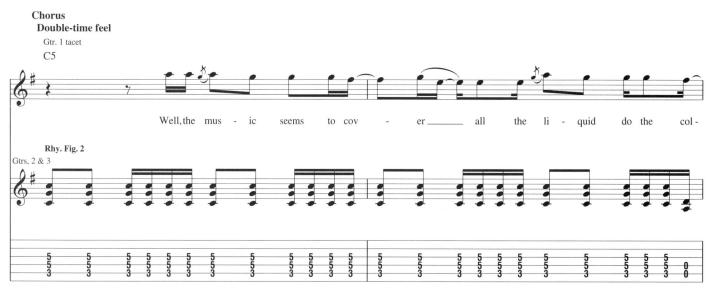

Well, the mus-ic seems to cov-er ____ all the li-quid do the col-

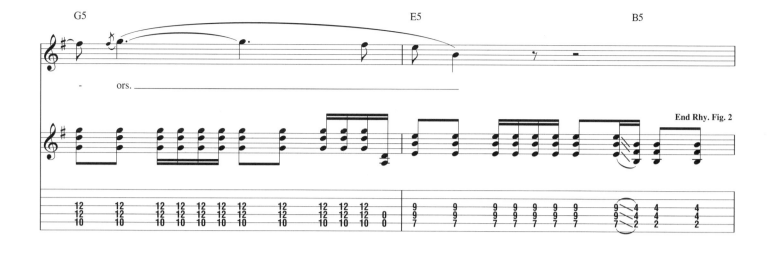

G5　　　　　　　　　　　　　　　E5　　　　　　　B5

End Rhy. Fig. 2

- ors. _____

Gtrs. 2 & 3: w/ Rhy. Fig. 2

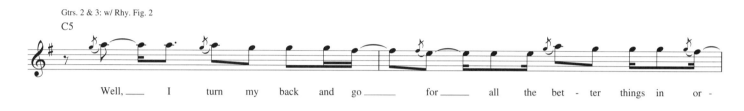

C5

Well, ____ I turn my back and go ____ for ____ all the bet - ter things in or -

End double-time feel

G5　　　　　　　　　　　　　　　E5　　　　　　　B5

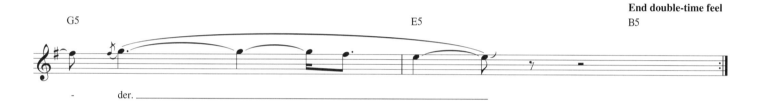

- der. _____

Interlude
E5
Riff A
Gtrs. 2 & 3

End Riff A

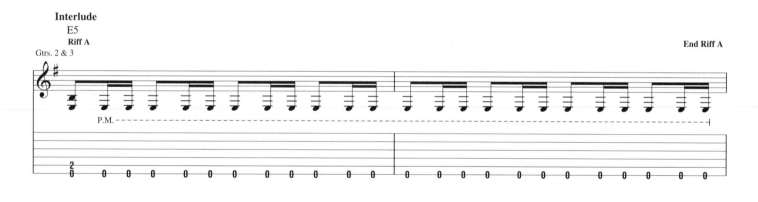

P.M. --------

Em　　　　　　　　　*D/F♯　　　　　　　G　　　　　　　Am
Gtr. 2

Gtr. 3

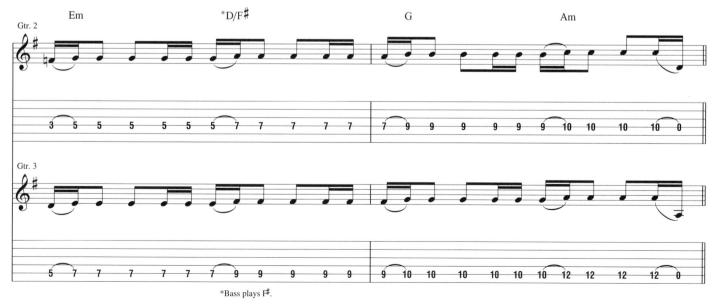

*Bass plays F♯.

Chorus
Double-time feel

Gtrs. 2 & 3: w/ Rhy. Fig. 2 (4 times)

Well, the mu - sic seems to cov - - er _____ all the li - quid do the col - ors. _____

_____ Well, _ I turn my back and go _____ for __ all the bet - ter things in or -

- der. _____ And ___ a gang - ster keep on tell -

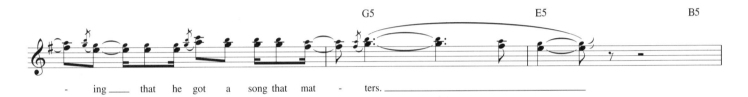

- ing ___ that he got a song that mat - ters. _____

So ___ I flip a coin to - wards __ him, __ thank you ver - y much for list - 'nin'. _____

Interlude
End double-time feel

Gtrs. 2 & 3: w/ Riff A

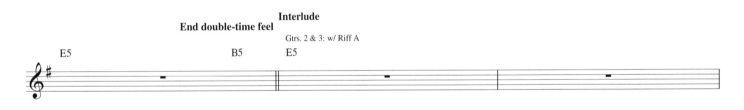

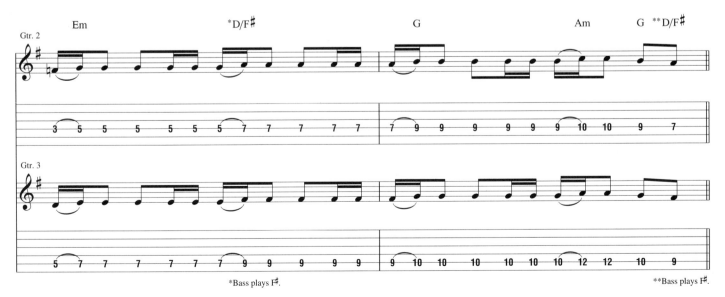

*Bass plays F♯.   **Bass plays F♯.

Outro

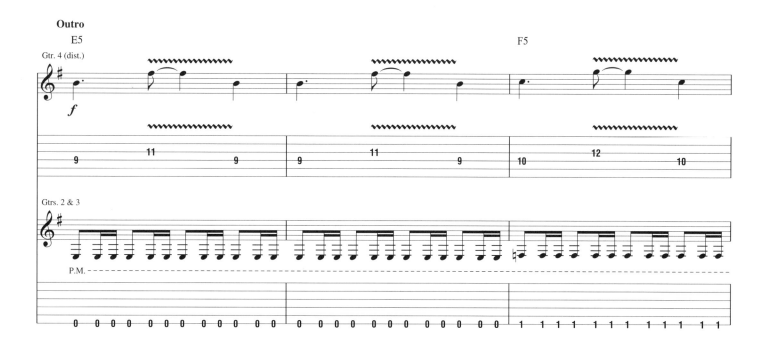

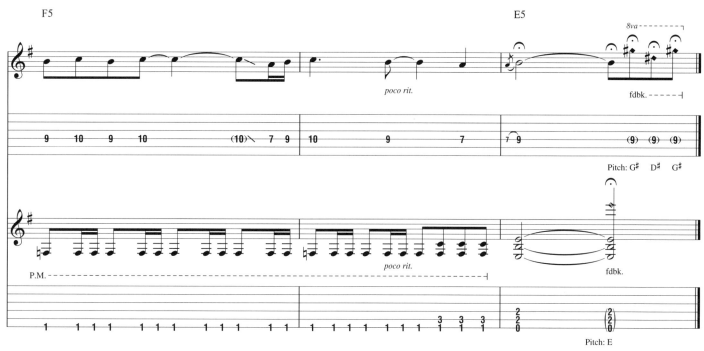

Survival

Official Song of THE LONDON 2012 SUMMER OLYMPIC GAMES

Words and Music by Matthew Bellamy

Gtr. 2: Tuning:
(low to high) A♭-E-A-D-G-B-E

Intro
Moderately slow ♩ = 82

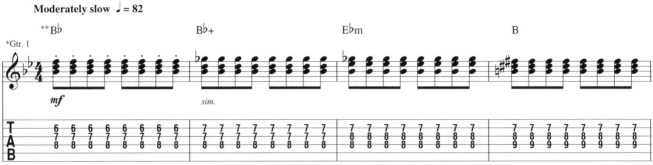

*Piano arr. for gtr.
**Chord symbols reflect overall harmony.

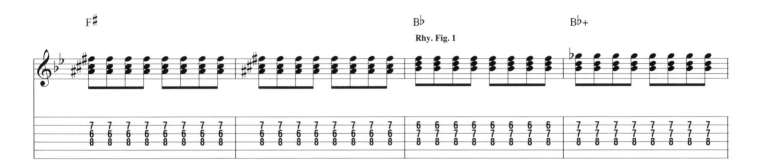

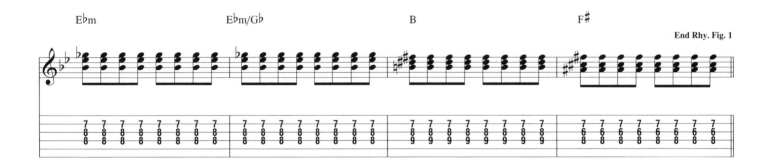

Verse
Gtr. 1: w/ Rhy. Fig. 1 (2 2/3 times)

1. Race,   uh, life's ____ a race   that I'm gon-na ____

____ win. ____   Yes,   I'm gon-na ____ win.   And I'll light the ____

Interlude

*Sung behind the beat.

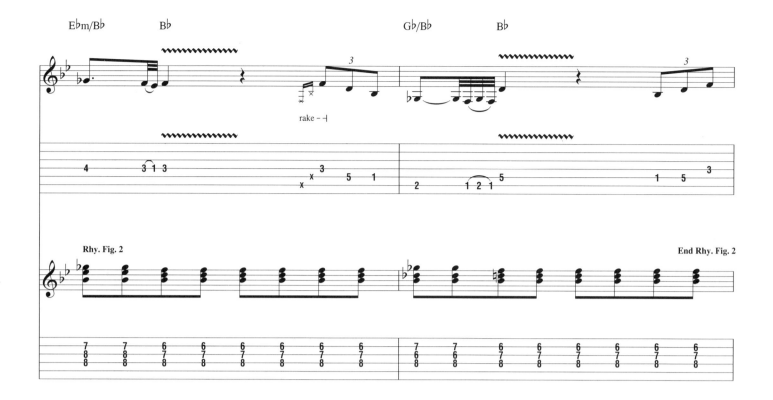

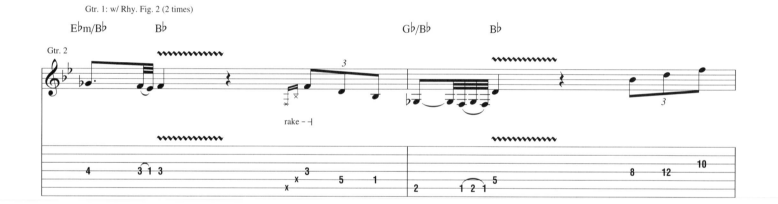

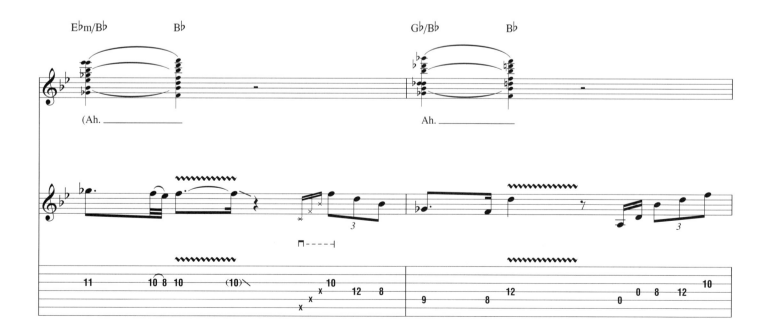

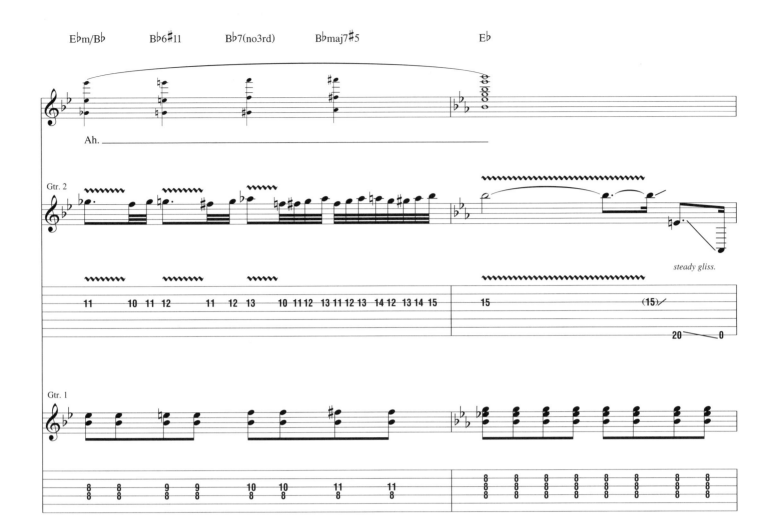

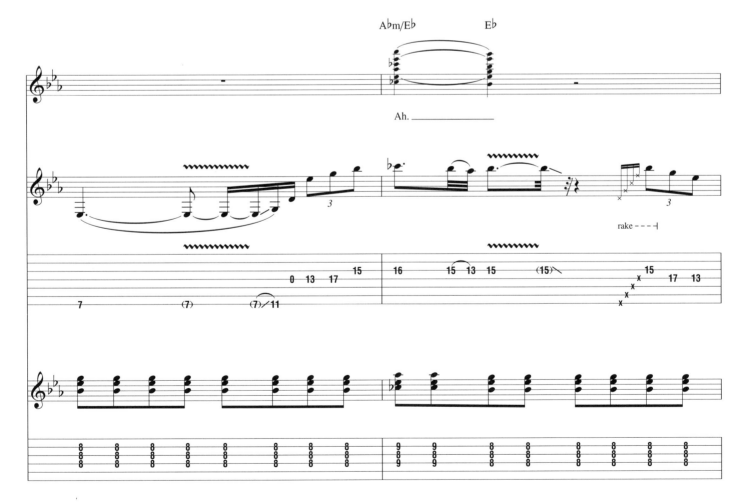

Verse

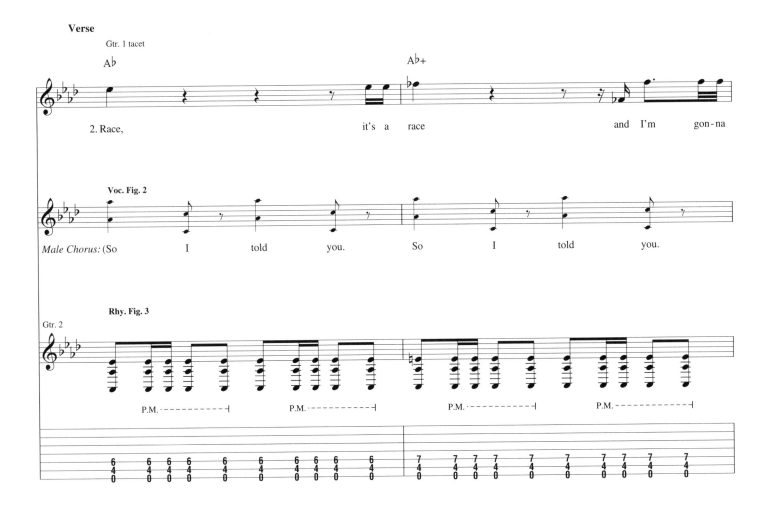

End Voc. Fig. 2

fuse   and I'll   nev - er   lose.   And I   choose to   sur -

So   I   told   you.   So   I   told   you.)

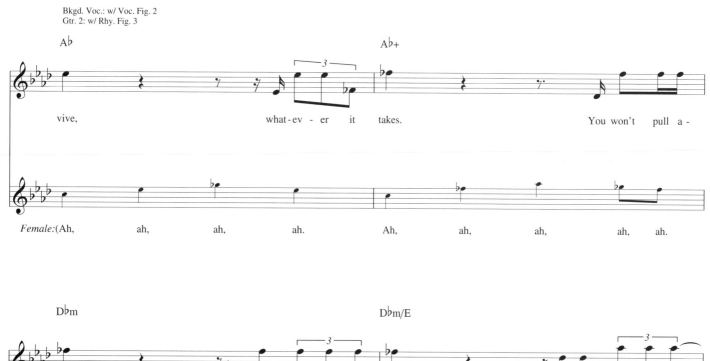

Bkgd. Voc.: w/ Voc. Fig. 2
Gtr. 2: w/ Rhy. Fig. 3

vive,   what - ev - er   it takes.   You won't   pull a -

Female:(Ah,   ah,   ah,   ah.   Ah,   ah,   ah,   ah,   ah.

head   'cause I'll   keep up   the   pace.   And I'll   re - veal   my ___

Ah,   ah,   ah,   ah.   Ah,   ah,   ah,   ah,   ah.

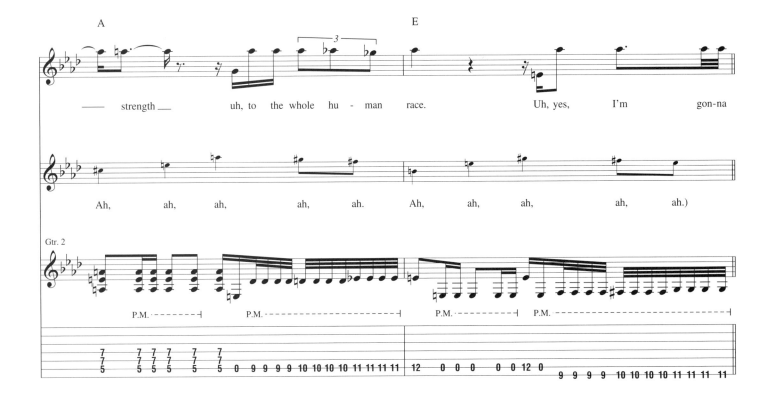

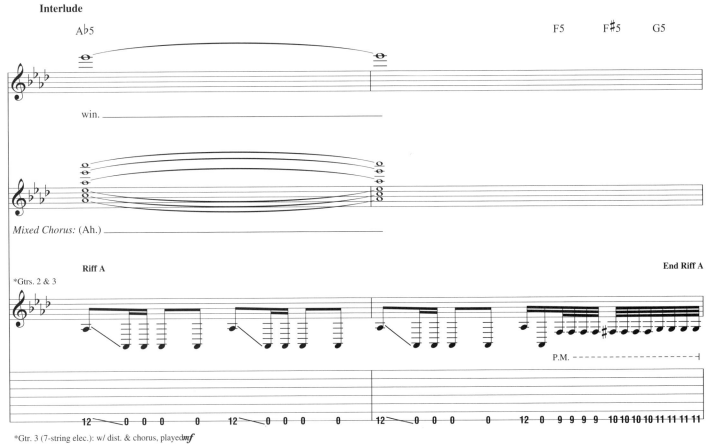

Guitar Solo

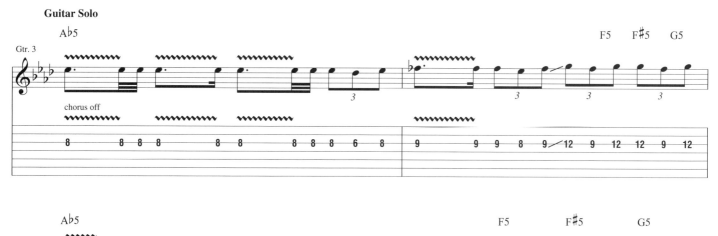

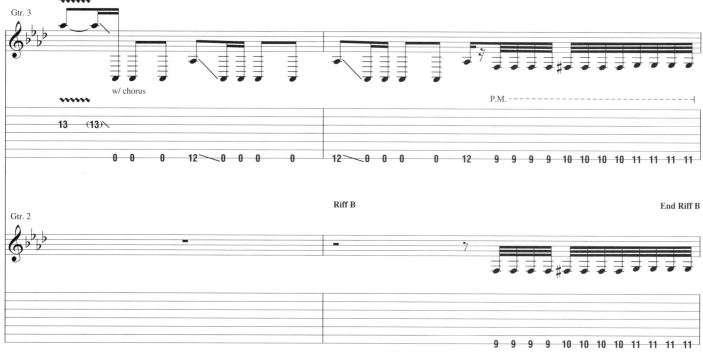

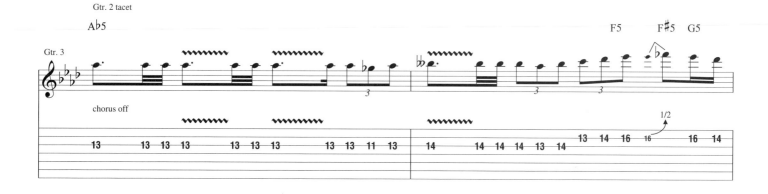

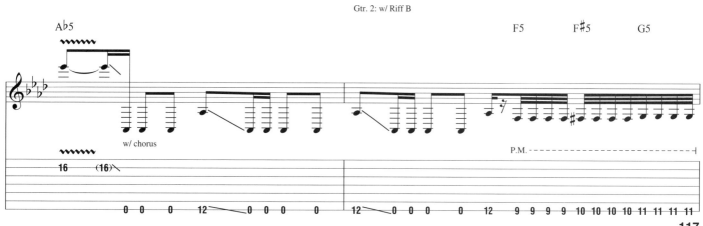

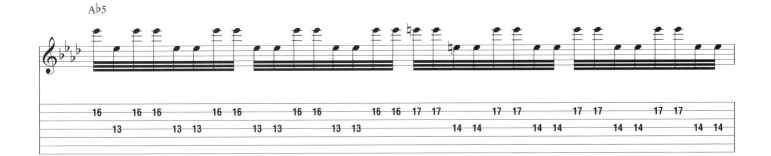

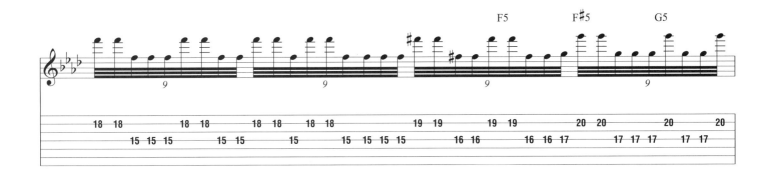

Gtr. 2: w/ Riff B

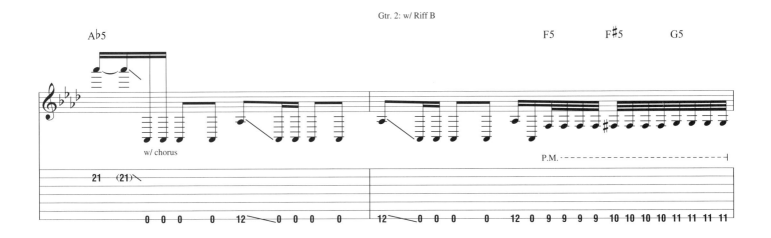

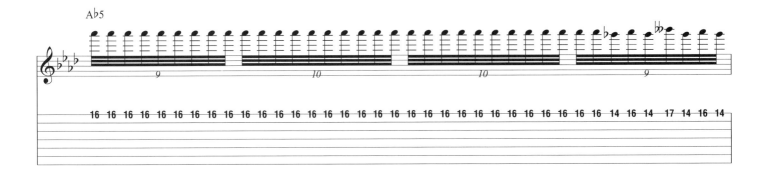

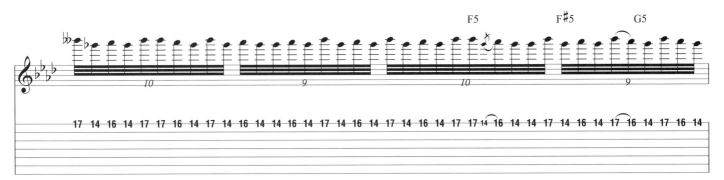

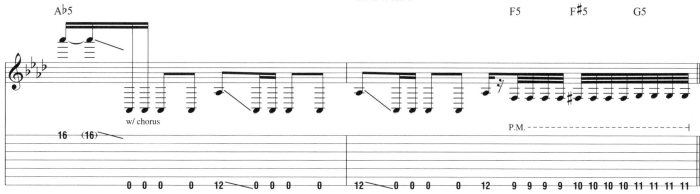

Outro

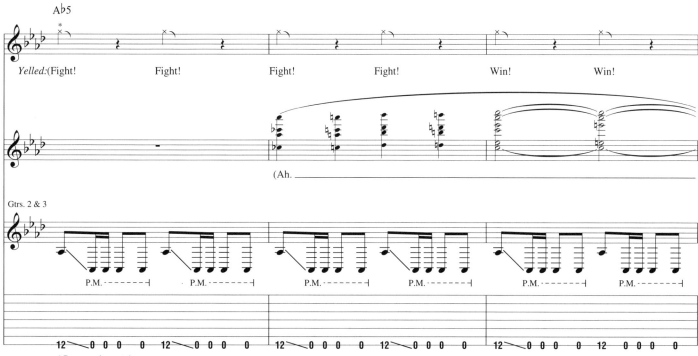

*Gang vocals, next 4 meas.

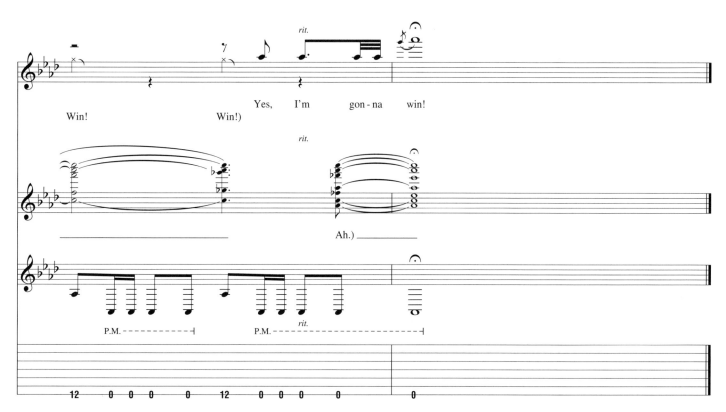

from Alex Clare - *The Lateness of the Hour*

Too Close

Words and Music by Alex Claire and Jim Duguid

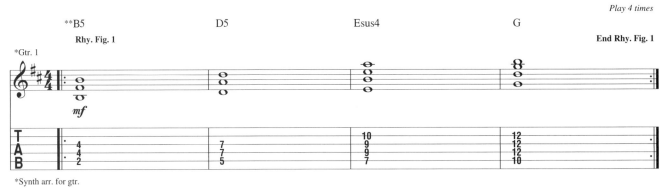

At the end of it all ____ you're still my __ best __ friend. __

But there's some-thing in-side that I need _ to re - lease. ____

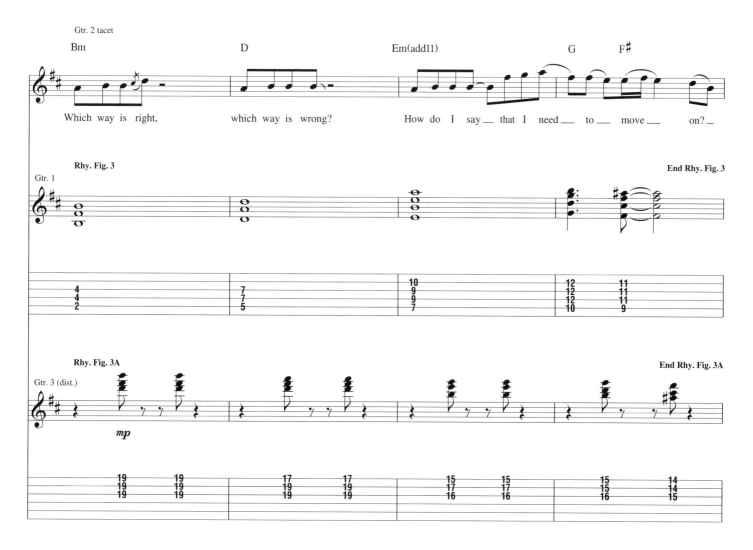

Which way is right, which way is wrong? How do I say __ that I need __ to __ move __ on? __

Gtr. 1: w/ Rhy. Fig. 2 (1 3/4 times)

Bm   D   Em   G   F#

noth-ing to say,   noth-ing to do.   I've noth-ing to give.   I must leave ___ with - out ___ you. ___

Gtr. 1: w/ Rhy. Fill 1

Bm   D   Em   G   F#

You know ___ we're head - ed sep - 'rate ___ ways. _____   And it

Chorus

Gtr. 5: w/ Riff A (last 6 meas.)

N.C.   E5   G5   F#5

feels   like   I   am   just   too   close ___ to   love ___ you. ___

B5   D5   Em   G   F#

There's ___ noth-ing   I ___ can   real - ly   say. _____

Rhy. Fill 2   **End Rhy. Fill 2**

Gtr. 4

```
15        15        15    14
17        17        15    14
16        16        16    14
```

Gtr. 4 tacet
Gtr. 5: w/ Riff A (last 6 meas.)

B5   D5   E5

I   can't   lie   no   more,   I ___ can't   hide   no   more. ___ Got   to   be   true   to   my - self. ___

G5   F#5   B5   D5

_____   And   it   feels   like   I   am   just ___ too   close   to   love ___

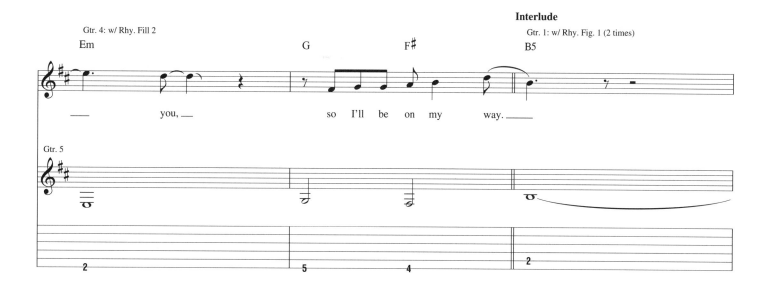

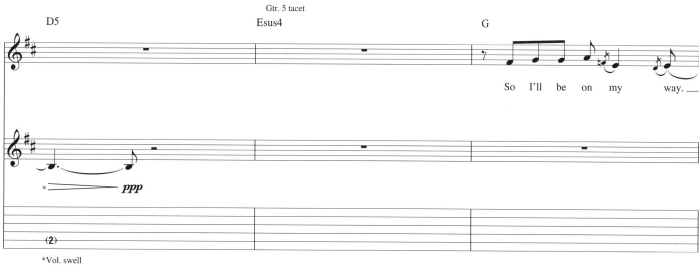

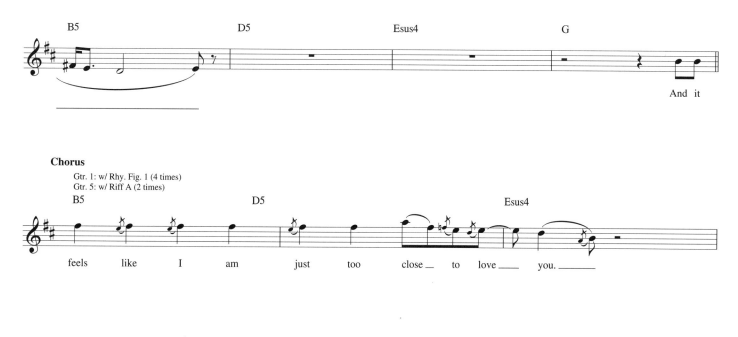

GUITAR NOTATION LEGEND

Guitar music can be notated three different ways: on a *musical staff*, in *tablature*, and in *rhythm slashes*.

RHYTHM SLASHES are written above the staff. Strum chords in the rhythm indicated. Use the chord diagrams found at the top of the first page of the transcription for the appropriate chord voicings. Round noteheads indicate single notes.

THE MUSICAL STAFF shows pitches and rhythms and is divided by bar lines into measures. Pitches are named after the first seven letters of the alphabet.

TABLATURE graphically represents the guitar fingerboard. Each horizontal line represents a string, and each number represents a fret.

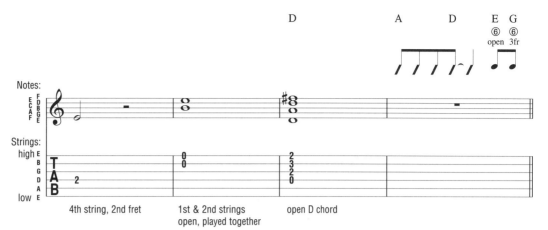

4th string, 2nd fret

1st & 2nd strings open, played together

open D chord

Definitions for Special Guitar Notation

HALF-STEP BEND: Strike the note and bend up 1/2 step.

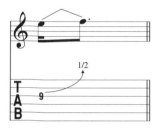

WHOLE-STEP BEND: Strike the note and bend up one step.

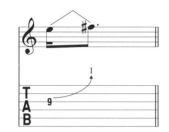

GRACE NOTE BEND: Strike the note and immediately bend up as indicated.

SLIGHT (MICROTONE) BEND: Strike the note and bend up 1/4 step.

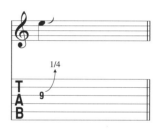

BEND AND RELEASE: Strike the note and bend up as indicated, then release back to the original note. Only the first note is struck.

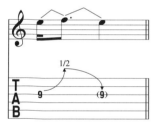

PRE-BEND: Bend the note as indicated, then strike it.

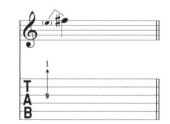

PRE-BEND AND RELEASE: Bend the note as indicated. Strike it and release the bend back to the original note.

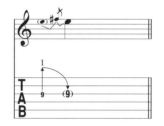

UNISON BEND: Strike the two notes simultaneously and bend the lower note up to the pitch of the higher.

VIBRATO: The string is vibrated by rapidly bending and releasing the note with the fretting hand.

WIDE VIBRATO: The pitch is varied to a greater degree by vibrating with the fretting hand.

HAMMER-ON: Strike the first (lower) note with one finger, then sound the higher note (on the same string) with another finger by fretting it without picking.

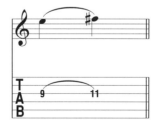

PULL-OFF: Place both fingers on the notes to be sounded. Strike the first note and without picking, pull the finger off to sound the second (lower) note.

LEGATO SLIDE: Strike the first note and then slide the same fret-hand finger up or down to the second note. The second note is not struck.

SHIFT SLIDE: Same as legato slide, except the second note is struck.

TRILL: Very rapidly alternate between the notes indicated by continuously hammering on and pulling off.

TAPPING: Hammer ("tap") the fret indicated with the pick-hand index or middle finger and pull off to the note fretted by the fret hand.

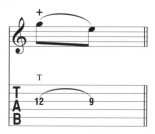

NATURAL HARMONIC: Strike the note while the fret-hand lightly touches the string directly over the fret indicated.

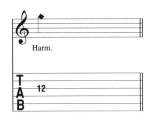

PINCH HARMONIC: The note is fretted normally and a harmonic is produced by adding the edge of the thumb or the tip of the index finger of the pick hand to the normal pick attack.

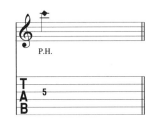

HARP HARMONIC: The note is fretted normally and a harmonic is produced by gently resting the pick hand's index finger directly above the indicated fret (in parentheses) while the pick hand's thumb or pick assists by plucking the appropriate string.

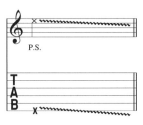

PICK SCRAPE: The edge of the pick is rubbed down (or up) the string, producing a scratchy sound.

MUFFLED STRINGS: A percussive sound is produced by laying the fret hand across the string(s) without depressing, and striking them with the pick hand.

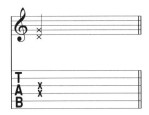

PALM MUTING: The note is partially muted by the pick hand lightly touching the string(s) just before the bridge.

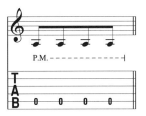

RAKE: Drag the pick across the strings indicated with a single motion.

TREMOLO PICKING: The note is picked as rapidly and continuously as possible.

ARPEGGIATE: Play the notes of the chord indicated by quickly rolling them from bottom to top.

VIBRATO BAR DIVE AND RETURN: The pitch of the note or chord is dropped a specified number of steps (in rhythm), then returned to the original pitch.

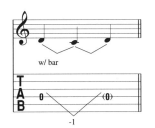

VIBRATO BAR SCOOP: Depress the bar just before striking the note, then quickly release the bar.

VIBRATO BAR DIP: Strike the note and then immediately drop a specified number of steps, then release back to the original pitch.

Additional Musical Definitions

> (accent)	• Accentuate note (play it louder).	
^ (accent)	• Accentuate note with great intensity.	
• (staccato)	• Play the note short.	
⊓	• Downstroke	
∨	• Upstroke	
D.S. al Coda	• Go back to the sign (𝄋), then play until the measure marked "*To Coda*," then skip to the section labelled "Coda."	
D.C. al Fine	• Go back to the beginning of the song and play until the measure marked "*Fine*" (end).	

Rhy. Fig.	• Label used to recall a recurring accompaniment pattern (usually chordal).
Riff	• Label used to recall composed, melodic lines (usually single notes) which recur.
Fill	• Label used to identify a brief melodic figure which is to be inserted into the arrangement.
Rhy. Fill	• A chordal version of a Fill.
tacet	• Instrument is silent (drops out).
	• Repeat measures between signs.
	• When a repeated section has different endings, play the first ending only the first time and the second ending only the second time.

NOTE: Tablature numbers in parentheses mean:
1. The note is being sustained over a system (note in standard notation is tied), or
2. The note is sustained, but a new articulation (such as a hammer-on, pull-off, slide or vibrato) begins, or
3. The note is a barely audible "ghost" note (note in standard notation is also in parentheses).